Praise for *Electri*

MW00654871

"Energy determines how we show up every day, our attitude and even our productivity. *Electric Life* will teach you how to harness your best self and become someone who is passionate and excited about what they do. Bill G. Williams's fun spirit and engaging stories will keep you hooked from cover to cover!"

DR. MARSHALL GOLDSMITH, Thinkers50 #1 executive coach; *New York Times*-bestselling author of *Triggers, Mojo* and *What Got You Here Won't Get You There*

"Bill G. Williams's *Electric Life* will challenge you to hone your self-awareness, unearth your own brilliance and discover the powerful difference you can make."

DR. TASHA EURICH, organizational psychologist; *New York Times*-bestselling author of *Insight* and *Bankable Leadership*

"Bill G. Williams's twelve microsteps provide important insights into who we are, why we are who we are, what we do and how we do it—with a focus on lifelong learning, continuous improvement and growth. You'll learn how to lead with humility, love and service, and to work together to create value for the greater good. Very electrifying!"

ALAN MULALLY, former CEO, Boeing and Ford

"Life is both simple and difficult. Electric Bill shows you the dance steps to make it joyful."

MICHAEL BUNGAY STANIER, author of *How to Begin* and *The Coaching Habit*

"Many people don't 'show up' fully. This is true in life. This is especially true in business. If I've seen one trait that is always prevalent in the most successful people who I've come into contact with, it's their ability to bring their whole self into everything they do. It's not a secret. It's not something reserved for certain types of individuals. It's accessible to all of us. If you're not sure how to show up fully, here's Bill G. Williams's *Electric Life*! He even breaks it all down into twelve microsteps. You can take twelve microsteps, can't you?"

MITCH JOEL, author of *Six Pixels of Separation* and *Ctrl Alt Delete*

"If you want to believe in your brilliance, support your brilliance. Read this book, rekindle your fire and make your life electric."

RON TITE, author of *Think. Do. Say.: How to Seize Attention and Build Trust in a Busy, Busy World*

"If you are feeling stuck and want to re-energize your career, let Bill G. Williams guide you effortlessly through the easiest steps that will make the biggest change. You can do it, and *Electric Life* will show you how!"

LAURA GASSNER OTTING, *Washington Post*-bestselling author of *Limitless: How to Ignore Everybody, Carve Your Own Path, and Live Your Best Life*

"No one brings more passion to their life and work than Bill G. Williams. *Electric Life* is an entertaining and hyper-practical book that will give you the motivation and ideas you need to imbue your life with more focus, energy and joy."

DANE JENSEN, CEO, Third Factor; author of *The Power of Pressure*

"There are so many great nuggets in Bill G. Williams's book—in the tips and in the text—that I found myself often nodding (energetically!), feeling reminded and enlightened by the many performance messages that apply to all ambitious people."

MARNIE MCBEAN, OC, OLY, three-time Olympic champion; Team Canada's 2020 Olympic chef de mission

"Bill G. Williams's incredible energy is tightly woven through every page of *Electric Life* as he shares simple, yet unconventional steps and ideas to be a better you day after day. His rich stories are relatable, digestible and easy to approach as the world we navigate seems to be anything but. For anyone who is looking to add more electricity, energy or happiness to their life, this book is a perfect place to start!"

ERIC TERMUENDE, author and keynote speaker

"This book is a game-changer. Whether you're an executive or recent graduate, you'll uncover actionable strategies that could transform your life. Bill G. Williams cuts through the noise, outlining twelve concrete steps you can take today to unleash new energy and be a more effective leader. Refreshing, helpful and thought-provoking, this book will guide you through the framework you need to live a more electric life."

SHANE FELDMAN, serial entrepreneur, keynote speaker and TV personality

"This book is utterly charming and seductively simple. You'll react by thinking, 'I can do THAT!' 'I SHOULD do that!' 'I WILL do that!' And we'll all be better for it."

LIANE DAVEY, author of *The Good Fight*

"The energy we project in the world is critical to our success. Each page of *Electric Life* is filled with great stories and practical insights to help you be the person who inspires others, generates passion and helps people be their best."

DR. VINCE MOLINARO, strategic leadership advisor; *New York Times*-bestselling author of *The Leadership Contract*

"Bursting with energetic game-changing expertise, *Electric Life* urges you to act with zest, intrepidness and heart."

DAN PONTEFRACT, author of *Lead. Care. Win.*

"A great read for leaders at all stages of their leadership journey! Electric Bill takes you on a personal and engaging journey through his leadership experiences and provides authentic concepts to 'show up' as the best version of yourself every day!"

EDWIN FRIZZELL, regional vice president, Central Canada, Accor; general manager, Fairmont Royal York

"*Electric Life: 12 Microsteps to Pay Attention, Be Brilliant and Go Deep* is a blueprint for teaching yourself to make your family, partner and work associates feel desired and appreciated. Bill G. Williams embeds the acronym SVI (special, valued and important) into your brain so you truly understand that effective communication results in effective relationships."

SHANE MCWEENY, hotel manager, Boston Park Plaza

electric

BILL G. WILLIAMS

LIFE

12 Microsteps to Pay Attention, Be Brilliant and Go Deep

PAGE TWO

Cataloguing in publication information is
available from Library and Archives Canada.
ISBN 978-1-77458-171-1 (paperback)
ISBN 978-1-77458-172-8 (ebook)

Page Two
pagetwo.com

Edited by Lisa Thomas-Tench and Amanda Lewis
Copyedited by Shyla Seller
Proofread by Alison Strobel
Cover and interior design by Fiona Lee

billgwilliams.com

CONTENTS

In everybody's life, at some time, our inner fire goes out. It is then burst into flame by an encounter with another human being. We should all be thankful for those people who rekindle the inner spirit.

ALBERT SCHWEITZER

INTRODUCTION

YOU CAN call me Bill. Born William Grant Williams, known as Billy Williams, in Fort William, Ontario. That's who my mother decided I was. But, by the time I was in grade seven, I became Bill.

When I was eleven, we moved from northern Ontario to Kamloops, British Columbia. Kamloops is the anglicized version of the Shuswap word *Tk'əmlúps*, meaning "the meeting of the waters." That year, I was part of the first class at the new South Sa-Hali Elementary School. Mr. Gardner, my grade seven teacher, asked what my name was, and I said, "I'm Billy Williams." That's the name my mom *really* chose—William was just what her best friend convinced her she should put on the birth certificate.

And he said, "You're too old to be called Billy, so we will call you Bill."

He didn't win any favours with my mother for that name change. But then Mr. Gardner asked me to deliver the school's opening speech and represent the students. I wrote out what I wanted to say, practiced in front of a mirror and brought as much energy as I could to the task at hand. I let myself get excited. Later, at the CFJC-TV station with some of my classmates, I told the whole of Kamloops about who I was. On television, no less.

Bill Williams. Someone new, my own person for the very first time. And my parents were very proud of me.

And now, I'm Electric Bill, as some people have defined me. That's because the question I get asked the most often is: "How do you always have so much energy? Sure, it's your job to energize crowds, but it's more than that!"

Since that first time I spoke in public all those years ago, I've been on television and on stages all over the world, and my approach hasn't really changed that much. Every year I address the crowd at The Art of Leadership, a conference designed to explore the intersection between art and business. I engage audiences as my profession, but I still prepare in the same way I did when I was in grade seven. I write out what I want to say, practice in front of a mirror and bring as much energy as I can to the task at hand. I let myself get excited about what I'm going to do and who I'm going to meet.

My whole life I've worked in predominantly female-dominated industries like travel and retail banking, and I'm a gay man. I've looked at the world differently from many of my male peers. I see myself as a lifelong learner, which isn't true of many people, no matter their identity or job role.

Especially at work. And especially when it comes to understanding why we lose faith in ourselves and how we spend our time every day.

I made the choice to keep learning. We all get to choose who we are and how we represent ourselves, and how we learn from our good and bad experiences. In choosing our path deliberately and joyfully, we can discover and keep and even *build energy* to live with purpose. Our own purpose! It's not our experiences, but *who we are* that matters. I identify with and accept my role as Electric Bill, because I *want* to create and share my energy.

I have created a life infused with energy, my philosophy of what I call *the energy to live*. I've written this book because I know that we can all find our own energy to live, energy that is real and sustainable. An energy that allows us to find the value in our everyday lives, work, families and community. I can't literally give you my own energy, but I can tell you where my energy comes from, and how yours can grow.

In this book, I'm giving you twelve tiny steps forward. I'm calling them microsteps because they aren't huge life changes that will require hours of your time to master. Not one of these microsteps is particularly difficult. I want you to *gain* energy, not lose it in this process!

To find that energy, we need to pay attention, be brilliant and go deep.

This book is about *you*, and what choices you can make based on knowing where your energy balance lies *right now*. It's about who you are, and the disconnect between that person and the person you want to be. We need to talk about our energy burning out, versus having the energy to go and do what we want to do *now*. We absolutely can create enough energy working so that we feel good every day, and so we have the energy to go and play *after* work.

In fact, you *can leave work feeling like you have more energy than you arrived with.*

Hi, friend. I'm Electric Bill.

Who do you want to be today?

PART I

PAY
ATTENTION

1

FIND
YOUR
HURRICANE

The art of bringing
your whole self to work

MANY OF us have heard the legend that, engineering-wise, if you consider the weight of a bumble-bee in comparison to the size of its wings, it should be impossible for that bumblebee to fly. In 1934, a French scientist named André Sainte-Laguë made some dinner-table calculations on the ratio of bumblebee wings to their weight, and concluded that flight was physically impossible. Sainte-Laguë's story continues: no one told the bumblebee that it couldn't fly, and so it did. It's a beautiful tale, and a good lesson for us all.

But the story isn't quite what it seems. And, in fact, there's a better story about that little bumblebee that hasn't been told quite so often.

The fact is that bumblebees' wings are almost magic.

When bees fly, their wings flap in a rotating pattern known as *dynamic stall*. This pattern creates a little gap in the airflow around them, lowering the air pressure. In that air pressure gap, bumblebees' wings operate at the perfect ratio to their bodies' shapes and sizes.

Bumblebees are, in effect, tiny little hurricanes.

Bumblebees know exactly what they are doing. They know how to fly. They know how to perfectly spin the air around them so that they float. And even if a French scientist underestimated them, bumblebees don't underestimate their own power.

Bumblebees bring the energy of a hurricane to every single flower they touch.

All they have to do is show up.

WHEN I worked in a corporate financial services office, I had my team meetings every Monday. The first Monday of every month was my team's meeting with me; they brought the agenda. The second Monday of every month I met with members of my team for a one-on-one. Again, I had no agenda; I listened.

The third Monday of every month was an all-team meeting in which I gathered information for situation reports for my boss. The fourth Monday of every month I met one-on-one with my team members again, but this time, I created the agenda. One of the questions I asked was, "In the last month, what accomplishment were you the most proud of?"

The first time I asked that, everyone thought I was strange, and they didn't have an answer. So the next month, I asked again, "In the last month, what accomplishment were you the most proud of?" They were perplexed. "Yeah, that question again. And guess what? I'm going to ask it next month. So I really encourage you to come prepared to our meeting next month." So on our third consecutive meeting I asked them, "In the last month, what accomplishment were you the most proud of?"

And they told me. Finally I was able to get to the next step.

"Can I be abundantly clear with you?" I said to each of them, "I expect you to keep your resumé on the desktop of your work computer. And I would encourage you to add that accomplishment to your resumé. Right now."

There were many shocked faces that day. It felt like a very strange thing to be asked to do at work. No, I wasn't lining up the next round of corporate layoffs. I wanted my team members to be proud of what they had done, and proud of what was uniquely, perfectly them.

TIP: Keep a list of all your accomplishments—a *done* list!

How often have you seen a job posting and said to yourself, "Tonight I'm going to update my resumé" and then repeated that process every night, until an exhausted ten nights later you realize it's too late and say to yourself, "I guess I'm stuck here." I wanted my team to feel as if they could go to another job at another company, or *choose* to be in their current role on my team. By making that choice every day, they could bring their own energy to their work, not their daily grind.

You see, in the corporate world, a company can only pay for your body to show up. Your job is to show up and be ready to work on time, and to accomplish your tasks. In fact, everything else is a volunteer role: your emotional commitment, your passion, your innovative ideas. Even if those qualities are why they hired you in the first place, a company can't force you to feel intrinsically motivated. Why is it that companies keep trying to extrinsically motivate people with t-shirts and hats with the company logo? Coffee mugs and fancy water bottles don't motivate people to work harder.

No company can force you to feel good about what you're doing.

TIP: Always have your resumé on your desktop and up-to-date.

Part of the challenge is that we aren't like bumblebees. We're not doing the essential work that bees do, namely ensuring that the whole world runs smoothly, one granule of pollen at a time. We don't have that hardwired belief in our role at work, not usually. In fact, we're expected to believe that we have a "professional self" and a "personal self," and, at work, we're told we need to focus on one at the expense of the other. We're taught that work is hard and fun is only had after work is over. At the same time, we're told to count our blessings because at least we *have* a job. Or we're asked to ignore the myriad of grumbles around us, or the fact that, like so many people in this world, we took a job for pay rather than a career we love. And don't think that working through your lunch hour is going to get you out of the office any time sooner. No wonder it all feels like a grind.

But there isn't a *work you* and a *home you*.

There's only *you* and that individual needs to feel like their authentic self is truly seen in all spheres of life. We can't split the professional and the personal into separate entities. If each of these aren't nourished, cared for and energized, well, eventually we will fail in *both* spheres. We will suffer from an emotional overflow from home to work and work to home, a brutal spiral which progresses from bad to worse.

And where does that potential hurricane of energy go then?

Precisely nowhere.

TIP: Volunteer your ideas! Be *honest.*

Carol Dweck, in her book *Mindset*,[1] writes about two mental states: fixed mindset and growth mindset, which help to define our personalities. On the one hand, a fixed mindset assumes that our character, intelligence and creativity are unchangeable, as if they were engraved on a rock. A growth mindset, on the other hand, is based on the assumption that our life qualities can be nurtured and can change. When we choose to learn from our experiences, life can be a bit brighter and more filled with opportunity and joy. I absolutely believe in what Dweck is saying.

TIP: Maintain a growth mindset—
ask questions and diversify your thoughts.

But I also think we can start finding our potential hurricane even before we're really feeling up for a growth mindset.

We can start by just *showing up* in body, mind and spirit. When I say show up, I mean *be present*.

BODY: When you show up, are you approachable? Does your body language prevent connection, a connection which could be the source of not only collegiality, but also help and innovation to make your life easier?

MIND: When you show up, are you honest about what's bothering you? Do you talk about your ideas and communicate what matters to you?

SPIRIT: When you show up, do you have passion about who you are, what you are meant to contribute and whether you give a damn about any of this? Do you love what you're doing? No matter how small or simple it is, do you give it your all and do the best job you are capable of every moment?

None of these questions is meant to admonish you. Ideally, they allow you to pinpoint *what's working and not working*. If you're not showing up, nothing is wrong, but you may want to start asking yourself *what needs to change* so that you feel like you want to show up. Ask yourself: What is it about this job that I don't like? What is it I'm looking for in a job? What do I *love* to do? Showing up is at the heart of energizing ourselves to be who we really want to be. Can you show up for work, for your life, with your whole body, mind and spirit each day?

———————————

TIP: Remember *why*

you're passionate about your job!

———————————

Showing up is strapping into our own little hurricane of energy so that we don't sink. And we show up for ourselves first: not for our bosses, our friends or even our families.

We show up for ourselves so that we can float like bumblebees.

CHOOSE YOUR BALLOON

The art of making
your own luck

A N ANCIENT Zen story goes something like this.

An old Chinese farmer had one old horse that he used to plough his fields. One day, the horse ran away into the hills.

Everyone said, "We are so sorry for your bad luck."

The old man replied, "Bad luck, good luck, who knows?"

A week later, the horse returned with a herd of wild horses, which now belonged to the old man. Everyone said, "We are so happy for your good luck!" The old man replied, "Good luck, bad luck, who knows?"

While his only son was riding one of the wild horses, he fell off and broke his leg. Everyone said, "What bad luck!"

The old man replied, "Bad luck, good luck, who knows?"

One day, the army came to the village and took all the strong young men to be soldiers for the emperor. Only the old farmer's son was spared, because he could not fight with a broken leg. Everyone said, "What good luck!"

The old man replied, "Good luck, bad luck, who knows?"

The moral of this story is that human beings have a tendency to interpret events as either good luck or bad luck.

Often we do this unconsciously. When we interpret events as good luck, we're usually happy about an outcome. When something bad happens, we think of it as bad luck.

But there really isn't any luck. Not really.

There's just us, and how we perceive, use and represent what we experience in the world, and even who we are.

MY FATHER was born in England and my mother in Canada. I was raised with a stiff upper lip. And our family didn't talk about anything, so we seemed perfect on the surface. In fact, because my mother was an amazing seamstress and knitted well, the Williams family had matching plaid shirts and matching sweaters. She knit one sweater set for the family out of wool that looked like denim. Good luck, bad luck, who *really* knows? Even so, my mother's sweaters were the talk of the town, as were her hats on Sundays.

My father was a workaholic, an electrician by trade, and after he returned home from work, he'd go and repair the neighbours' washers and dryers and televisions. My mother, well, let's just say that she couldn't always be left alone at night because of her bipolar disorder. You might call this bad luck, for her or for the Williams family. But every one of us, and by that I mean all of us reading this book, can look back upon our pasts and look at old photographs, and relate to the idea that we put on a show when we're in front of a camera. (Like your friends on social media posting their perfect pictures!) At the same time, we understand that what's going on behind the scenes is absolutely different from the smiles on those faces in the pictures.

So yes, I learned how to put on a show along with the rest of my family. Like many kids who grew up in perfect-on-the-surface families, I tried to be the golden child so that our family problems would just go away. I navigated our family as purposefully as I could, pulling up a chair to the kitchen sink to wash the dishes so that I could receive a literal pat on the head. I believed that being a good boy meant that mommy wouldn't cry from her depressions. Back then it wasn't known as bipolar disorder—it was manic depression. I always tried to make my mother laugh whenever I could.

And by the time I was in grade seven, I conducted the school choir at concerts, acted in plays and, as you know from the introduction to this book, landed my first public speaking gig.

Good luck? Or the result of being the try-hard son of a hardworking dad and a mentally ill mom?

TIP: Good luck/bad luck: always question which it is and seek the other perspective.

We can all find an energy that doesn't rely on luck.

Think about a time when a friend invited you to their child's birthday party. Maybe you arrived a little too early, and you were roped into helping decorate and set up the room. Someone handed you some balloons to blow up. You picked a few in your favourite colours, stretched one out, and then filled your lungs with air and pushed as hard as you could to blow up this balloon. Just as you tried tying a knot to keep the air in, the balloon slipped out of your fingers and fluttered away. You blew it up again, but couldn't achieve that original pristine shape. The balloon looked completely different.

I believe our minds have the same qualities as that balloon. Our minds are neuroplastic, and once stretched by a new idea, will never return to their original shape.

In a similar way, we can make an impact on our own lives by choosing how we think, what matters to us and what will define and represent who we are in the world.

What happened before today really doesn't measure into anything unless we want it to.

———————————

TIP: Use your superhero power—be curious!

———————————

Today, right now, how can you intentionally choose your luck? Dial up your superhuman power of curiosity. Ask yourself:

- What are the events, workplaces or social groups where I feel engaged and valued for my contributions?

- Who is in control of the conversations where I feel seen and heard?

- How can I rethink my environment, even in the smallest way, so that I feel more alive and energized?

- What are the things I want to add to my life, to have an impact and change my balloon? What are the things I want to remove from my life so that they *don't* change my balloon?

- How can I get one per cent more comfortable in my role at work?

We can all find an energy that drives and revives us. We can do this if we are on the lookout for what represents who we want to be, who we *see ourselves being.*

Representing, actually *re-presenting,* who you are is about making decisions about what you can *gain* from both good and bad experiences. Lost your chance at a dream job but got a sexy short-term contract? Spent a lot of time and money on a graduate degree but realized you studied the wrong field? Won a prize to paraglide off a mountain, but were too scared beyond belief to use it?

Present what you've experienced to yourself in a new way. See it for what it is. And decide whether it's the right thing to shape your balloon and whether you're going to love it or lose it. You're allowed to let things go. For example, I loved the energy I gained from making my mother laugh, and kept on looking to use that energy throughout my life. The rest, well, it's a part of me, but I no longer need to lean into it. Understanding the ability to reshape your balloon is a real power that can make you feel nourished and brilliant at the same time.

This process doesn't rely on luck, but instead relies on your own unique, authentic brilliance.

Believe in your brilliance.

Believe in your light, your power, your intelligence, your drive and your ability to see your own balloon, flawed yet perfect and constantly changing.

3

"FINE" IS NOT A FEELING

The art of figuring out
what you feel

THERE'S A highway that crosses Canada from the Pacific to the Atlantic Ocean, called Highway 1. Most of it would be better considered a small road, one lane in each direction over the great plains of the Prairie provinces and around the northern reaches of Lake Superior, where I was born.

If you've ever been in the city of Toronto, however, you'll know that that poky, rambling asphalt turns into an eighteen-lane mega-freeway called the 401, one of the top ten busiest highways in the entire world. The average speed of a commuting driver ranges from zero, when the 401 turns into a relative parking lot at five pm, to a bracing 140 kilometres an hour when things really get moving. Toronto commuters like weaving in and out of traffic to find a sweet spot, until their lane gets backed up and they're on the move again.

As soon as you put a steering wheel in somebody's hand, the road becomes all about them, and only them. In fact, I once saw someone get out of her car in the middle of the 401 and walk up to the window of the driver of an eighteen-wheeler who had tapped her bumper just so she could scream at him more thoroughly. Why? That vehicle was her armour. She was like a knight in a jousting match with a big stick and a horse. People have this untested belief that they cannot be physically harmed if they're in (or, in her case, standing beside) a car, surrounded by steel and glass, even though we've all twisted our necks to see a crash on the side of a freeway more than once.

I'm not the only one who no longer drives in my adopted hometown. The 401 is a mess. I stopped forcing myself through those armoured warriors on the freeway because of how angry I chose to get when I drove.

I mean, it's traffic, right? It's normal. It's expected. I should be fine, right? But no, I felt like I owned the road. Why were all of these people in my way? Why were all of these people making me late?

HOW ARE *you*, really? Right this *very now* moment?

You're thinking, "Fine. I'm just fine, Bill!"

But be honest with me. Does saying "fine" feel like an energetic response? When's the last time you checked in with yourself and had a definitive, truly true, without-any-doubt answer to that question?

As a young man, long before I identified as gay, I married my female high school sweetheart. We had what I would say was a very normal marriage, but we were very young, and I hardly knew what to compare our marriage to at the time. She was nineteen when we wed. I had just turned twenty. And there's a chance I wasn't being totally honest about what I wanted, or, at least, I didn't *know* what

I wanted from a committed partnership after growing up in rural Canada where the choices were few and far between. When our marriage ended, seven years later, I saw a therapist for the very first time in my adult life, in an office in Vancouver. The therapist asked me how I was doing.

And my answer to her was, "Fine."

Yeah.

And she said to me, "Well, Bill, fine isn't a feeling. Are you happy, sad, glad, mad or angry?"

I couldn't answer that question, for a lot of now-obvious reasons. My confusion was, well, pretty run-of-the-mill. *Not* knowing what we're really feeling is, in fact, normal.

Dr. Tasha Eurich, a psychologist, wrote a book called *Insight*, and in it she says that, even on a good day, about eighty per cent of us are lying *about* ourselves and *to* ourselves.[2] It's normal for people to create the world we want to live in, *even if it's not real*. So when we're driving on an eighteen-lane mega-freeway, we might as well actually be in Elizabethan England on our trusty steed, rather than contemplating the 35,972 accidents that happen on the 401 each year.

That's why the worst part about not knowing what we're really feeling, Eurich says, is that the only lies for which we are truly punished are those we tell ourselves.

TIP: Check *in* with yourself—
how are you feeling?

So, before you can show up, you have to know yourself.

Feeling just fine, just neutral, about what's going on around you is, I believe, a form of lying to yourself. It's risking putting yourself into a mindset where you're not allowing yourself to see the whole picture of who you are.

And that's a risk I don't think serves anyone well at all.

Maya Angelou once said, "I've learned that people will forget what you said, people will forget what you did, but people will never forget how you made them feel." I take exception to this. People didn't *make you* feel anything. How did you choose to feel?

The author of *Emotional Intelligence*, Daniel Goleman, talks about how we need to understand other people's feelings and emotions so that we can communicate and interact with people more easily, especially at work.[3]

If you've ever walked into a room filled with tension thick enough to cut with a knife, you've likely met at least two people who are lacking in emotional intelligence. More than likely those people are not aware of how they're feeling, nor are they aware of the impact they're having on other people in that tension-filled room.

People who understand and perceive their *own* emotions are better at understanding other people's body language, tone of voice and facial expressions. Because we mirror other people's reactions, through emotional intelligence we can build a greater ability to understand ourselves and other people. We can do this through the practice of empathy.

And, in fact, new research mapping our brain functions shows that when we feel empathy for others, we learn faster.[4] It's a mindset that neuroscientists call *prosociality*. When we use prosociality at work, or, in other words, when we start our days and our conversations with emotional intelligence and empathy, we can develop new skills that have nothing to do with emotion. Simply put, prosocial brains are brains that are primed for adding new ideas and new functions to our toolbox, from completing calculus equations to taking on horseback riding for the first time.

But remember, we're aiming to do a better job at understanding and perceiving our *own* emotions before anything else. We need to learn emotional intelligence from the inside out.

So let's make it personal.

And let's do it through three simple choices.

CHOICE 1: Thumbs Up or Thumbs Down?

What kind of day is it? Thumbs *up* or thumbs *down*?

There's a fine line between a thumbs-up "fine" and a thumbs-down "*FINE*," isn't there? You can hear the *edge* in someone's voice when it's the latter. Ask yourself: Am I okay? Am I good? Choose one: thumbs up or thumbs down. It doesn't take a lot to tap into which one you're feeling right now. So go ahead and make that sign, the one you're authentically feeling right now.

CHOICE 2: How Much?

Ask yourself: how much of a thumbs-up or -down feeling am I sensing in my body right now?

If you gave yourself a thumbs up, are you woo-hoo-running-up-and-down-the-halls-high-fiving-people great?

If it's a thumbs-down day, how bad is it? Are you just over the edge of neutral, or is it brutal and you need to go take a kickboxing class right now because that's how bad it is? Name that. Make an analogy if you'd like, or give a real (or fantastical) name to how much you're feeling at the moment.

CHOICE 3: What's the Impact?

Ask yourself: What's the effect I'm having on other people when I'm feeling like this?

Are you self-aware enough to realize the impact you have on others? Do you care? Sure, we know there's a difference between our emotions and how they are expressed, and we also know that there are ingrained social values and expectations that help us understand other people's emotions. But the reality is that we *act* differently than we think, and being aware is the best way to understand whether we're creating energetic potential or just draining energy, from others *and ourselves*.

MANY YEARS ago in my work life, I had a manager who had the ability to make people *very* uncomfortable. The five paces between his desk and the table where we met were among the most awkward steps I've ever taken. The pauses he took between questions and answers represented the loudest silences I've ever heard. After those meetings ended, I would feel uncomfortable for hours. And the worst part was that I thought he used that discomfort intentionally to try to motivate me, and our entire team.

But negative motivation has never worked for me, and it doesn't work for most people. His efforts certainly didn't make me run back to my desk and get that project finished on time or under budget, they just demoralized me and devalued me.

Was that manager aware of his effect on me and on others? Probably not at all. I did not tell him, either. And even if he was aware—I believed he didn't care. It was his strategy to put us down so that he could feel superior!

So let's tie this back to our goal of understanding our own feelings and how they have an impact outside of our own heads. We need to know ourselves, and to know our effect on others, so that we can live, learn and connect, and so we don't unintentionally create barriers to cooperation.

———————————

TIP: Why are you choosing to feel your feelings? Can you choose to feel a different way? Focus on what makes you feel the way you want to feel.

———————————

There's a flip side to knowing how we're feeling. Being self-aware helps us to build emotional strength so that we can manage our discomfort and sit with it. We can't always be the best version, or even a good version, of ourselves, especially under pressure. Moving away from discomfort seems easiest, whether it's the manager who is trying to motivate us with a stick rather than a carrot, or us trying to manage our own challenging emotions. And all of this causes stress on our bodies as well as our minds. We're never going to totally avoid that discomfort. But we can manage our stress by mapping out where we are emotionally, and allowing ourselves to notice what's happening as a result.

You are your own best witness.

When we allow ourselves to notice and feel what we are truly feeling, we can do something with our observations. We can take a walk, have a cup of tea, reach out to a friend and laugh over a shared memory. When we're not taking stock through our three choices, we might not know what path to take to feel better. Trust that, first and always, you owe yourself empathy.

And then, remember that you owe yourself radical candour.

As author Kim Scott writes, radical candour is allowing yourself to say what you really mean at work, rather than glossing over facts to save face and please the higher-ups.[5] I think we should be also radically candid with ourselves. We need to be honest about how we're feeling so that we can be emotionally intelligent about our own life experiences, and so that we can see other people for who they are. But also so that we can ask for what we want!

We need to be honest about how we're feeling in order to get to the juicy parts of life. Connection. Innovation. Excitement. True joy.

So.

How are you, *really*?

PART II

BE
BRILLIANT

PLUG IN

The art of tapping into
your potential

SOMETIMES, YOU just have to go to the movies.

A friend of mine—let's call her Elle—snagged a pretty great job right out of business school at a major multinational consumer products company. Think Nestlé, Unilever, Procter & Gamble: the kind of place where there are high expectations, an entrenched hierarchy, and a huge team. Elle was excited, and her energy was high when she arrived on the scene. But pretty soon, she realized that face time, just being there, was more important than how long she took to get her work done. In fact, people regularly worked from seven am to seven pm, arriving a few moments before their bosses did and leaving a few minutes later than them. It was a rolling arrival and exit, those at the top left the earliest, and entry-level employees like Elle waited to leave until the lights were turned off by the cleaning crew.

The work wasn't particularly strenuous. In fact, it was pretty rote. Elle knew that if she put her head down, she could finish everything on her to-do list in about three hours each day.

But what Elle also noticed was that people a few levels above her were taking very long lunches, like three- and four-hour lunches, especially when patio season rolled around. Part of the job required site visits and meetings with suppliers and buyers, so almost everyone on Elle's team left for some portion of the workday, every day.

About three months into her job, Elle walked past a cinema multiplex for the hundredth time when she was out buying her lunch.

On the hundred-and-first day, she opened the door to the movie theatre instead of going back to work.

The thing is, Elle was tired of playing the face-time game, and, in fact, the work itself was getting tiring. The culture was a drain on her energy. So every few days, she took herself to the movies, bought popcorn and a Diet Coke instead of lunch and put her feet up on the chair in front of her.

Elle didn't lose her job.

No one noticed she was gone at all.

And she gave herself a break from her cream-coloured cubicle for a few hours so that she could go on pretending she was working hard when she sat there for the ten more hours she was expected to be there.

I wasn't surprised when she quit.

In that culture, Elle's work energy was completely out of sync with who she was, and what she wanted to do with her time.

TIP: Decide what *your* desired
results are, at work and in life.

Your energy can be converted to different forms, but it can't be created or destroyed.

That's not just my point of view, being Electric Bill and all. That's the first law of thermodynamics devised by the French natural philosopher Gabrielle Émilie Le Tonnelier de Breteuil, Marquise du Châtelet, in 1740. She built on Isaac Newton's premises and discovered the power of kinetic energy. Émilie, as she was known, suggested that when we are not using our energy, it's still right there, in potential form.

We can do anything with our energy.

In our story, Elle's company wasn't using her to her true potential. And it looked like the same was true for the company's other employees as well.

These employees' potential energy was dormant. And in that dormancy, the employees felt tired, underwhelmed, bored and, ultimately, they burned out. All of that fire within them was burning up their *will*.

A lot of Elle's story is about the difference between *management* versus *leadership*. I'd hazard to say that management doesn't know what it wants until it gets what it *doesn't* want. And even then, management *still* doesn't know what it wants. Elle's company shouldn't have been encouraging face time over work time. And, in fact, if she could get all of her work done in three hours, there's nothing wrong with that. We can manage a project, we can manage a budget, we can manage a schedule, but we cannot manage a human being. *Leaders*, however, are abundantly clear about what good performance looks like. If Elle and her colleagues were achieving their goals, then new goals can be set, so that their energy isn't wasted.

How can work culture breathe life into people? Think about this. If you keep doing what you've always done, you'll get what you've always got. Plot that on a graph. What shape does it make? A flat line. If I took you to the hospital and you had a flat line, what would they tell you? You're dead! So many people talk about a song, book or movie that inspired them, but so few people can tell me what the word *inspire* means. The "spire" part means breath. "In" means, well, to take it in. So do you breathe life into people or suck the energy out of them?

TIP: What breathes life into you at work?

Tapping into your potential energy starts with plugging in.

Wherever you go, connect to *your* energy source. Recharge.

When I moved to Toronto, I wanted to get to know my new neighbourhood. I walked into the local grocery store and greeted the person in the floral department, asking about her day. I engaged with the person working the self-checkout, who was dealing with no end of problems, and wished them an easier day. I chose to give them my energy.

When I stay at a hotel with colleagues for a conference, the people I'm with tell me, "Billy, you go; you go check us in." And, sure enough, we get upgraded, snag a room on a better floor, or get a coupon for the restaurant or a late checkout.

When I give people a smile, when I engage in conversation, when I share eye contact with someone and learn something new about them, those experiences are rewarding for me. I'm not actually looking for a discount or a free daisy, I'm looking to build connections.

And that's when something magical happens.

It's all in how we approach our conversation. For me, it's giving a damn. Every time.

If you're going to be asking for something, whether at a store, at work or at home, what are you giving back in that environment? So, you want late checkout at the hotel? How are you treating the person who picks up the phone? I've got friends who will lie, intentionally, and say something like, "When I checked in, they told me I could check out at four o'clock."

"Who was it who told you this?" they're asked in return.

"Well, I don't know. Whoever checked me in."

Then it turns out the person who checked them in was the manager, who is standing right there, and knows my friend is lying. And my friend knows they are lying as well. What kind of energy exchange is that? Simply put, it's lowering the tone of the conversation.

I'm not insinuating that you'd lie under the same circumstances. I'm guessing you're better than that. But we all can remember a time when we weren't quite aboveboard in order to game the system. Maybe it was justified! Maybe it was the easiest thing to do at the time. But when we look back at those moments, did we actually feel good afterward? How much do these low-energy transactions affect us, for hours, days, even weeks after we have them? And what do those low-energy transactions do to the hope we feel on a daily basis?

TIP: *Give* the energy you want to receive!

Do you remember why you got into the industry you're in right now?

Let's say you're a schoolteacher. You probably started doing this work because you wanted to make an impact in your community, or because you really loved learning from Mrs. Patel in grade six. Add to that the fact that you get two months off in the summer. But maybe, especially in these harrowing times, you've become a bit jaded about online learning.

But there are still reasons to be passionate about teaching. Why is teaching so important to you? Or accounting? Or completing electrical repairs?

We gain energy when we're honest, transparent and truthful.

When we give something in exchange for others' energy, no matter how small it may be.

When we give a damn.

So if there are still reasons for you to be passionate about your work, start there. Remember these reasons, practice them, put energy into them. In the beginning you were excited, passionate and happy to get that job offer. What was the offer? Why were you excited, and can we relight that fire? Or is it time to realize you *must* move on to what you're passionate about now in order to build your energy to live?

That's how you are going to get that energy back, and be energized at the end of the workday. When you plug in, the return on your energy investment is always beyond belief.

BE
SELF-FUL

The art of filling
your own tank

LOVE EXPLORING the mysteries of what it means to be human. Some people indulge themselves in conspiracy theories or documentaries about aliens. Some read thousand-year-old poetry, others watch *Real Housewives* with a bottle of chardonnay.

I pick up a deck of cards.

Chandra Mohan Jain, later known as Osho, was an Indian mystic who inspired the teachings inside the Osho Zen Tarot. It's a pretty famous deck of cards, and it comes with a book of wistful explanations of all of life's foibles. Now, to be clear, I don't think that tarot cards can predict the future, and neither did Osho. Interpreting the cards is about gaining an understanding of the here and now based on the wisdom of Zen Buddhism. It's a look at life through the lens of a great thinker and soul searcher.

When I look at the cards, the meaning is simple: what I notice tells me something about *myself*.

Here's why. The card in the Osho Zen Tarot that is the most meaningful to me is the number seven in the suit of water, called Projections. Looking at that card, I've come to understand that we all have our own fantasy movie about our lives: what we think is true or false, what we think we know, love or hate. This fantasy movie takes hold when we are not fully aware of our own desires, aspirations and judgements. Because we aren't aware, we don't perceive reality. It's a little like being in a movie theatre, staring at the screen, when the projector is behind us, holding the reel of film. Our minds are like that projector facing outward, so what we see, feel and understand are often projections as well.

And that's meaningful, because when we see something we love in our work, our friendships and our day-to-day lives, it's also a projection of our *selves*.

Ask yourself, what am I projecting outward?

When I see something in somebody else that I love, it's often something that I love about *myself*. And when I see somebody who's being a jerk, it's reminding me of times when I was a jerk. Either example is a chance for a new *a-ha!* moment. And a chance to notice what's in the way of feeling my feelings, finding my hurricane and plugging in.

In fact, self-recognition is the beauty of allowing yourself to imagine what's possible and fully move into a growth mindset that you have the capacity to build, because it inspires you to show up.

DON'T THINK of noticing yourself, and, indeed, putting yourself first, as sel*fish*.

In fact, it's critical to your own life to be *self-ful*.

My mother once said to me, "Billy, don't be selfish, right? It's rude to be selfish. But you should always be self-ful."

Why? Because the in-flight adage about putting on your own oxygen mask first is true, and given my mother's own struggles, I think she was wisely caring for me in sharing that important piece of advice. But I don't think that adage goes far *enough*.

Putting on your oxygen mask is a survival tactic.

We have to go beyond survival mode if we want true, big energy.

TIP: Take care of yourself—put on your own oxygen mask first.

Earlier, we talked about emotional intelligence. We know for a fact that emotional intelligence is crucial for effective leadership in the workplace. That's because people rarely make decisions based on rational thought, no matter how hard they try to create a barrier between their emotions and their work. Real emotions have a real effect on individuals in the workplace, even under the normal stress and pressure of an average job. Emotional intelligence allows us to deftly create alignment between the goals and abilities of people by decreasing the friction that emotions, personalities and conflicts can cause.

That's all well and good. But we have to be emotionally intelligent about ourselves, not just other people.

To be emotionally intelligent, we all need a high degree of self-awareness. Self-awareness is the process of investing in *our own* personal growth, and becoming conscious of how we have an effect on the world around us. How we *project* who we are onto others. This requires time to reflect on what matters, and on how our perceptions influence what we do and how we interact with others.

The ability to shift our focus away from that big cinema screen comes as a natural consequence of self-awareness.

Getting ourselves into focus happens when we are clear on how we use our energy investment, and how we can better see the life we want to have. This is also how we develop a growth mindset, even within life's challenges, and develop resilience, an ability to respond gracefully to whatever comes. We become an upgraded version of ourselves and start to identify the times when we're at our best. We learn to cultivate joy, and be more intentional about our happiness.

There's nothing wrong with being self-serving.

Think about this. How are you building an effective relationship with yourself?

We're all a little bit complicated. We often feel like we have to dig deep to discover the ability to peel back the layers of the onion inside of us. And there's nothing wrong with that! But sometimes building an effective relationship with yourself is about going with the connections that are already *there*. Connections with *what is meaningful* to you.

There was a time in my life where I *just knew* that I wanted to work at Disney. But then I also wanted to work for Delta Hotels, and I wanted to work for an up-and-coming airline as well. What attracted me to these companies? What did they have in common? Their customer service philosophies, for a start. I thought those places were really cool, but, in the end, I never did get to work at any of them. But the companies that I chose to work for probably weren't too dissimilar from them, at least in terms of corporate culture.

What these companies also had in common was *me*.

No, I'm not being self-centred. I'm being self-*ful*.

The commonality between these potential workplaces was that their customer service philosophies had an outward, customer-centric orientation. And *that's* what I loved. And *that's* what I wanted to connect with. The idea that work could be centred on *people*.

These jobs weren't about the company, they were about who *I* was, what *I* valued and what *I was willing to spend time doing*.

Having an effective relationship with myself was about truly understanding what mattered to me and what didn't. It wasn't about words on a job description, but what made me feel good at the end of the day. Acknowledging my human needs made me more intrinsically motivated to engage in my work, and to choose what was right for me.

When you're happy with your life choices, you're involved. And involvement breeds commitment! You'll be passionate about clocking in every morning.

But the opposite is also true.

If your fire has gone out, then find a new fire. Begin the journey to find the *you* that *you want to be*. And consider, has the fire *really* gone out? Maybe you've lost the flame, but the embers (the deep original passions) are still there.

Can you breathe life and flames back into those embers or do you need to ensure the fire is out, for safety's sake?

It's a very short distance, that journey to what you want to be. But only if you build a connection to *what is meaningful* to you and you alone.

So where do we start?

Simple. Body, mind and spirit. We've got to feed these parts of us. Heal them. Honour them every day.

TIP: Get a good night's sleep; know how your body works best. Stay hydrated.

The evolution of my life's work, and my ability to be energized, started when I began taking care of my body. Respect for *my* physical self meant setting my alarm clock for physical breaks all day long, whether it was a few steps around the block or a few minutes on a bike. (Respect for *your* physical self might look somewhat different!) I used to work so hard that I would end up feeling sick, parked on my couch, helping no one, least of all myself. When I take some downtime, sleep, look at my nutrition and nourishment, and remember to check in with how my body is coping with everyday stresses, I feel better.

The same goes for my mind. When I feel my emotions rise, I stop and ask myself how I can tend to those feelings. Is there a wound that I still need to heal? Can I appreciate and acknowledge the growth that I've already experienced? What do I need to change to feel a little more comfortable in my own skin?

And as for spirit, I always remember that my body is on loan, as is my mind, but my spirit, that's what carries on.

This is really, really, really important.

What's the legacy you want to leave behind? What do you want to be known for? How do you want to spend the precious time that you have? What have you *not* done that you really *want to do*? Do you have the energy to do it?

TIP: Challenge yourself: What kind of energy are you leaving in the room?

You know when you've walked into a room with some-body who put on a little bit too much cologne, and the smell lingered even after they left the room? That's how I see my spirit. And I'm not talking about the Drakkar Noir your friend wore in grade ten. I want my spirit to fill a room up so much that, even after I leave it, the room still has a positive buzz and energy.

And I want that for you, too. I want you to be self-ful. I want you to feel as if you, and only you, can make the rules for your body, mind and spirit.

I want only you to get to decide who you become.

POWER YOUR CURIOSITY

The art of finding
your superhuman self

IT'S THE post-industrial age, so let's pretend we've cloned some sheep.

Dolly and Molly are our two clones. They both have the exact same capabilities and the exact same competencies, which means that they can produce the exact same work. We've sent them to work at our widget plant.

One day, Dolly and Molly are conscientiously making widgets; by two o'clock in the afternoon, Dolly is finished the ten widgets that management expects her to make. So Dolly is finished for the day.

Molly, however, has only completed six of her widgets. Her lambs needed her about halfway through her workday, and her mother-in-law gave her a call to bleat, and Molly never really got back on track.

What does management do? They don't only push back on Molly, because the reality is that Dolly and Molly's manager only cares about getting that total of twenty widgets finished at the end of the day. They decide they need all hooves on deck. So the manager returns to both Dolly and

Molly and says to each of them, "You need to make two more widgets."

So now, Dolly has made twelve widgets, while Molly has only made eight widgets.

The next day, what does the manager expect? The manager expects that both Dolly and Molly are each going to make ten widgets, despite Molly's tardiness the day before. That's what normally happens, isn't it?

But in actual fact, by their decisions the day before, management has taught both Dolly and Molly that they shouldn't work fast or get their work done by two o'clock. In actuality, Molly was rewarded for having slowed down. If either sheep finishes faster than the other, then they're going to be asked to do more. As a result, Molly ends up slowing down even more, but so does Dolly.

By two o'clock, there are only twelve widgets finished between the two sheep, leaving their manager eight short of expectations, even fewer than the previous day. Management decides they're going to have to clone another sheep, Polly, just to get the minimum amount of widgets produced each day.

And that's only one way people become disengaged, and deenergized, at work.

TIP: Know what you want and be honest, transparent and truthful about it.

From my own experience, I have clued in to the fact that when I'm in an environment or culture that doesn't recognize and reward me for my contribution, I *will* disengage. So, I intentionally choose to only become a part of work cultures where I *can be* engaged.

But I didn't get clued in easily. It wasn't until I was in the workforce for quite a few years that I learned one critical thing.

To gain energy, we have to dial up a superhuman power of curiosity.

In this sheepishly silly example, Dolly and Molly get what is going on through instinct. They're using Molly's experience as a template for their future behaviour, and copying what resulted in lessening her workload.

But we need more than just instinct to be truly self-ful.

Neuroscience shows us that most of what we do is influenced and controlled by the subconscious mind. We live on a kind of autopilot, which is both a good thing and a challenging thing. Autonomous processes are running in the background, and they help us navigate the repetitive parts of life, like driving a car, making phone calls and picking up our favourite foods from the grocery store.

Our familiar choices are made over and over again, and they become legacy patterns. We repeat these patterns at home and at work.

Often, these legacy patterns extend to our personality and other life characteristics. Genetic memory, collective frequencies of others around us, personal habits, what was taught to us, all of these aspects of life become repeated and ingrained.

Habits are our comfort place.

And let's face it: managers can take advantage of this habit orientation. Management is the part of the working world that deals with processes, budgets, schedules and so on. In fact, if you have had a life partner, you've likely experienced management even if you've never been given that job title. Every day after work, you go home at night and see your partner sitting on the couch. You've both had a busy workday. And you say, "Sweetie, what do you want for dinner tonight?"

And they say, "Oh, honey, anything you want."

"Okay, great. Well, let's order a pizza."

"I had pizza for lunch today."

"Okay, what do you want then?"

"Well, anything you want, except pizza."

It's a rabbit hole energy-suck.

As we learned earlier, management doesn't know what it wants until it gets what it *doesn't* want, and even then it still doesn't know what it wants. That's why I can manage a budget, I can manage a schedule, but I cannot manage a human being. Human beings will manage themselves, so long as they've got clearly defined goals or objectives or know what the performance standards are that they have to meet. And that's why managers corral us into creating work habits, standard operating procedures and policies from which we don't usually stray until we're given reason to think differently, as Dolly did when Molly stopped working so hard. Leadership is different. Leadership is about inspiring people to feel good at work, and offering abundantly clear ideas about what good performance looks like.

But, regardless of whether we're more of a Dolly or a Molly, we are *more than the sum of our habits!* And, perhaps even more important to realize: *we are more than the sum of our job duties.*

WHAT I know for certain is that having fun is central to life, and central to building our energy.

Cultivating fun is a core part of being human, and yet many of us are not enjoying our work in the slightest. It's okay to laugh and do silly things at work, and if we are never feeling that joy, there's a problem. It can get to the point that we'll do anything to avoid the work we're paid to do, either consciously or subconsciously. And yet our bodies are on loan, as are our minds; our spirits carry on. But we perform so much of our jobs out of habit that we're not getting curious about what matters to each of us.

TIP: Gamify your work—make it *fun!*
Reward your desired behaviour!

And the reason to pay attention and use our superhuman power of curiosity is because not every manager is going to be the leader we need, and, indeed, not every company we work for will be capable of creating a fun, engaging and truly leadership-oriented culture. In fact, research tells us that the only thing that can predict our engagement at work isn't what our bosses are doing.

What makes work fun and worthwhile (and, by the way, what makes life worthwhile), is *alignment* between our values and what we do. And alignment really has only two factors to consider: meaningfulness and work-life balance.

We can find meaning in our work when we have the autonomy to make decisions, when we have confidence in our own work, and through our own sense of psychological safety. We find work-life balance when we have the ability to shape our own futures and how we spend our time, reaching a level of intrinsic motivation that feels comfortable.

We need to lean into our superhuman power of curiosity, and refine what we want to do and where we need to make energy-giving changes. Ask yourself...

- What am I doing out of habit?

- Do I *really* like doing it?

- Do I feel vulnerable to constant critique from others or from myself?

- Am I feeling *managed*, rather than *led*?

- What might I do differently?

- How would it feel to try on a different approach?

All of these questions require you to be self-ful rather than aiming to meet your employer, partner, friend or even your pet dog where they are. And though these questions may feel daunting, they aren't hard questions to answer.

We human beings are inherently curious machines, and we can do this.

If we choose to use our superhuman power of curiosity, we by no means ensure we will avoid discomfort and challenges along the way. That's a given.

TIP: *Ask* the questions—be curious!

What using this power does ensure is that we can and will make choices that feel good. We may find the path we've been looking for so that we ultimately have the potential to experience true joyfulness and all that it offers.

If we don't use it, we'll never get that chance.

CELEBRATE MIS-TAKES

The art of living
your human life

MIS-TAKES, NOT mistakes, are new chances and opportunities for learning, in however many takes you need. Kids, for example, will take a chance on almost anything. They are energy personified. They'll fling themselves off a swing set and sing a solo in front of strangers. They're not frightened of being wrong or falling down. In fact, they want to fall down. They want to get muddy in a rain puddle and mess up their clothes. For kids, water balloons are still a *thing*, as is slime, in both of its natural and sparkle-enhanced forms.

As adults, we know that if we lose this sense of fun, and if we're not prepared to be wrong, we'll never come up with anything original, innovative or groundbreaking. It's not usually fun to participate in a stereotypical brainstorming session at work, for example, and yet our companies pressure us to amaze them with new ideas that are supposed to *disrupt the market* by the energetic force of their originality.

By the time we get to be adults, most former kids have lost their capacity to have fun.

Why?

We've become frightened of being wrong.

We're worried we're not as good as other people.

We stigmatize mistakes. In fact, we're now running education systems where mistakes are the worst thing you can make. Standardized tests are the norm.

We're educating people out of their creative capacities.

For all of these reasons, the late Sir Ken Robinson, who passed on too early, believed that building our capacity for creativity was as important as literacy, and we should treat it with the same status. Robinson was a British author, international advisor on education, the director of the Arts in Schools Project and professor of arts education at the University of Warwick. I had the privilege and pleasure of working with him in Toronto.

Except that our time together didn't go quite as planned.

Talk about mistakes.

SIR KEN ROBINSON contracted polio at age four, and as a result, his legs were physically different from each other. He wore a special shoe, and, when needed, he preferred to ride around in an electric scooter. His mobility was important to him. His disability did not prevent him from travelling around the globe.

MISTAKE #1: Arrangements had been made for a car to pick Robinson up at the Royal York Hotel and bring him over to the Metro Toronto Convention Centre. The car didn't show up. He ended up taking an Uber after realizing no one was coming to get him.

MISTAKE #2: We made *very specific* arrangements to have a scooter ready for him at the Metro Toronto Convention Centre, but for whatever reason, they brought in a wheelchair.

Everything ground to a halt.

We couldn't put the sponsor who was going to introduce Robinson in front of that crowd without knowing how long Robinson would take to arrive and how long it would take to get him a scooter.

Someone turned to me and said, "Bill, you're going to go out and you're going to just … stall. Fill the time until we signal you with the countdown timer. He's on his way."

I jumped out onto the stage, feeling alone and underprepared. There just wasn't enough time to get everything sorted perfectly, but the backstage team had the countdown timer at centre stage so that I would know how long I had to riff. When Sir Ken Robinson arrived and his scooter was ready, the sponsor would come out on the stage, and we'd be good to go.

I did what I normally did: connected people. I reviewed what the previous speaker had talked about to ground the crowd in their learning that day. I asked the crowd to share their key insights with their seatmates, and shared a few of my own. I thought I only had seconds left for patter.

Then, all of a sudden, I looked down at the countdown timer and it said thirty minutes.

I ran through all of the options in my head. What do you do on stage for thirty minutes when you've got no content? You've got no speech? This situation really isn't that different from standing in front of thousands of people naked.

And then, in a split second, I desperately looked down again and saw the timer flip back to five minutes. 4:59. 4:58. And I glanced to the side and saw Sir Ken Robinson waiting in the wings, smiling, the sponsor ushering me to stand down.

TIP: Make mis-takes. Just do it.

Making mistakes is *normal*. Normal! It's a mis-take—a chance for a second take—not a *problem*. No one should read my anecdote about the Robinson event and tsk-tsk the venue managers or the sound techs or whomever was in charge of that countdown clock. And yet we have a tendency to want to go deep on every opportunity to worry or criticize or, ugh, *debrief*.

I'm not saying we can't aim to be efficient, but we actually *aren't artificially intelligent*. We're *regular* intelligent, and we're flawed. And those flaws don't just make us cute and unique, they make us *adaptable*.

Robinson taught me that every education system on earth has the same hierarchy of subjects. At the perceived top of the pile are mathematics and the sciences.

Then the humanities, like economics and sociology and education.

And at the bottom are the arts.

Even within the arts, there's a hierarchy! Art and music are normally given a higher status in schools than drama and dance. There isn't an education system on the planet that teaches dance every day to children the way we teach them mathematics.

Why? Our public systems of education, as we know them, came into being to meet the needs of industrialism: making stuff in factories back in Queen Victoria's time. So what we have valued over centuries is rooted in two ideas. Idea number one, that *the most useful subjects to teach are those which help us work*. And the second idea is the concept of *academic ability*, namely taking tests well, which has really come to dominate our view of intelligence.

All of this has come to mean that many highly talented, brilliant, creative people underestimate themselves, because the thing they were good at wasn't valued at school, or may have *even been stigmatized*.

IN CREATIVE work, whether brainstorming at an accounting office or dancing with the Bolshoi or designing a Tesla, mistakes can lead to innovation and change.

But even more important, mistakes are part of *living a human life*.

I remember a time when people used to say that it wasn't professional to bring your personal life to work. Those same people also said: don't take your professional life home because your family doesn't need that baggage. Take it off before you walk through the front door.

How can we be human beings when we're never allowed to just *be*?

All of what makes us human has to come to work.

All of what makes us human has to come home as well.

All of what makes us human is perfect in its imperfection.

Sometimes we need to get over old expectations and just *remember who we are at our core*.

I know that I'll be okay on a stage in front of a thousand people when the speaker isn't there. You need to know that you've done everything that you need to do to prepare yourself for every single day *just by being alive*. If you've shown up, you've already done the work.

TIP: Discover new and better

ways of doing what you've always done.

You can be your creative, adaptable, mis-taken, fully human and fully normal *you*. Making mistakes and muddling on.

And knowing that things are going to be okay is what allows us to take a deep breath and save our energy for something else.

8

PRACTICE PAUSITIVITY

The art of
taking a break

BACKSTAGE IS the heart of a presentation. It's where the scene is set, microphones are attached to collars and tested, and everyone at a big event meets each other. People rush and mill around, checking tablets and paper lists, holding their hands to their headphones to hear a little bit better amidst the frenetic movement.

Backstage at The Art of Leadership event in Toronto, I met the man I was about to lead onto the large main stage. At that time, Joe Biden was the former vice president of the United States, and he was as congenial as you would imagine. He stopped to get a photo with me as I set up how I was going to introduce him, and tried to get my words just right to warm up the crowd.

Behind us, there was more commotion than usual. The production company had a huge backstage set-up for the former vice president, but they probably overdid it. Despite the big names treading the boards that day, we were essentially a group of speakers with PowerPoint presentations. We needed the lights to come up and our cues from the audio booth, but our presentations weren't rocket science.

That's why, at the last minute, right before I was to walk out on the stage, any kind of commotion did not bode well.

At The Art of Leadership, the day typically begins with a video. As event staff play the video, loudly, they dim the house lights so the crowd knows that the show is about to start. This time, however, the production team tried to roll the opening video, and it crashed.

They started the opening video again, and it crashed. Again.

The production team scrambled and then decided to instead play an audio file introducing me to the stage while the audience took their seats.

They rolled that and, again, it crashed.

They looked at me with the fear of impending doom in their eyes, as Biden just stood there, smiling.

"Just go out there," the stage manager implored me, hoping I could salvage this for everyone.

But everything that could possibly go wrong next was running through my head. Everything's just crashed. "Is my PowerPoint going to work?" I asked.

"I don't know." The stage manager shrugged.

"What do you want me to do?"

"Just go out there; start the show!"

I walked out, smiling just like Biden, and managed to get some laughs as I introduced myself.

"Are you excited today, or what?" I said to the crowd. "Because former Vice President Joe Biden is here!"

And then I just told the truth.

"Imagine the excitement backstage," I admitted to the crowd. "We roll our opening video and it crashes. We roll our opening video again and it crashes. We roll the audio introduction of me, and it crashes. So, here I am, your host, Bill G. Williams!" Then I told them the Billy a.k.a. William Grant Williams from Fort William story from the introduction to this book.

TIP: Discover the truth and say it—own it.

I was present in that moment, and even when all the technical systems around me were failing, I was still able to show up and gain the trust of the people in front of me, because I didn't pretend that everything was going perfectly. I was able to focus on what mattered; I looked out at that audience and knew in my core that they were excited about Joe Biden being there, and that I would manage to survive, and even laugh about this event sooner rather than later.

SUSAN DAVID, who wrote the wonderful book *Emotional Agility*,[6] says that forced false positivity is actually toxic positivity. What she means by this is that saying a situation is manageable, not a problem, or even wonderful when it's really *not*, is a big deal. When we pretend that everything is okay, it may sound innocuous on the surface, but it can have a significant impact on mutual trust, comfort and even our mental health.

False positivity is basically gaslighting-lite.

And every one of us uses false positivity! It allows us to deal with our own discomfort at the expense of someone else's. For example, think of a time when you shared something difficult with someone, like the fact that you decided to divorce or your dog died, and that person insisted that everything was going to be okay. Plenty of fish in the sea. So many shelter dogs needing a family. In essence, they're glossing over your sadness and forcing you to remain hopeful because they are uncomfortable dealing with your pain.

The same is true for smaller and bigger falsities. When my father was near the end of his life, he would spill water or make a mess and I would tell him, "It's okay, Dad." Then one day he responded: "It's NOT okay! I'm dying!" I wasn't acknowledging the reality of his situation and how hard it was; his okay and my okay were two different things.

When I was treading water on stage, stating the obvious about our technical difficulties wasn't a big deal, but it probably felt like a relief to the audience. Telling the truth gave us all a story to share about our day. It also saved us from collective embarrassment. We could laugh about it and relieve the tension.

Think about the impact of toxic positivity in the workplace. What happens when we're expected to tell our peers and bosses that our latest and greatest strategy is working when it's not?

When the emperor is not wearing clothes, we have to throw him a towel.

The bottom line is that human beings don't benefit from having their hard feelings and challenges shut down, and they shouldn't need to perform happiness to make others comfortable around them. This reinforces the idea that we all have to act perfectly at every moment, and that we can never be messy if we want to be loved.

In 1587, Pope Sixtus V formally established the position of *advocatus diaboli*, Latin for devil's advocate. During the process of deciding who and who would not become a saint after they died, it was up to this Catholic Church–appointed official to call into question a candidate's saintliness. The Pope decided that there were far too many souls being considered for sainthood, and there was more than a little chance that corruption played a role in this plethora of perfect people.

Routing out possible corruption wasn't a particularly enjoyable task for the advocate; the role looked for natural explanations for alleged miracles, and brought forward human and selfish motives for deeds that had been reported as heroic virtues. The advocate's duty was seen as difficult but necessary.

Even today, we need to be intentional about routing out false positivity.

I used to want to repel negative people, but now I adore them. I could repel them if I want to. But what would be the benefit?

I want people to be honest with me and feel comfortable doing it. Without hearing others share their ideas, my ideas can't grow. I am actually thrilled by negative people because, for example, I can show them my presentation and ask them to tell me what's wrong with it and what they would do to fix it. Human beings are hardwired to solve other people's problems.

I want to lean into that.

HOW DO we learn to invite this kind of open honesty?

For me, it starts with *paus*itivity.

When we learn how to pause and observe, and take it all in, we can be grateful for what we have. If we try to see things from someone else's point of view, we might better understand everything that they have to offer. Pausitivity is a chance to slow down and *conserve* our energy for a moment.

In fact, reflection, according to the experts, gets us one step closer to realizing our passions at work.

TIP: Take a pause and observe, whenever you want to, to make things better!

Neurological research shows that active self-reflection, where you take the time to reflect on who you are and what matters to you, allows people to build connections between old and new ideas. At work, this kind of mindful approach can directly improve performance on the job.[7] Reflecting on what's possible and bringing many different viewpoints into the mix allows people to make better decisions, and can directly lower costs, because it makes it easier for people to learn from their experiences.[8]

Pausitivity can start with others. People become communities when they know each other's stories, and are more aware of each other's potential, opening up doors to creativity, imagination and entrepreneurship.[9]

Pausitivity can also help to calm our monkey minds.

Buddha believed that we live with a constant barrage of chattering thoughts rambling through our minds, like drunken monkeys. Our lives are not just full, but overfilled, with tasks, responsibilities, the media and more. Our goal is to quell our own drunken monkey minds and all of the chaos on which they thrive. But we all are susceptible to that monkey mind, and its constant hunt for answers and the next big thing.

TIP: Focus on what you *know*—your life experiences and what you've achieved and experienced in the past. If you could do it then—you can do it now.

On that stage where I introduced Biden, my monkey mind could have made me nervous and freaked out, until I took a moment for pausitivity. My knowledge mind kicked in instead, and I thought to myself: "I've been on this same stage many times before; I've introduced myself and many important speakers before, and I can do this."

Pausitivity is a way to be self-ful in the most challenging of moments. We can learn the best lessons from negative people, adverse experiences and from looking within to take a moment, pause and really listen.

And then, we can get back to the truth and move forward.

PART III

GO
DEEP

9

SHOW ME YOU

The art of SVI

SAWUBONA IS an ancient Zulu greeting. It is used similarly to the Sanskrit word *namaste*, but its meaning is unique.

Sawubona means "I see you, so you exist."

After I first read about *Sawubona* in Susan David's book *Emotional Agility*, one of my clients who is South African and from a Zulu lineage explained it to me further. *Sawubona* suggests that we each represent our ancestors and our collective community interests; this word can help us to break down barriers, because it reminds us to recognize our whole selves.

In fact, Roche Mamabolo, founder of the LORA Centre for Innovation and Entrepreneurship in South Africa, gave a TED talk on *Sawubona* in which he makes the point that when we don't truly see each other, we are unlikely to appreciate each other. And truly seeing others is often missing from our relationships, especially at work.

"It is an invitation to a deep witnessing and presence," Mamabolo says. "We invite each other to communicate and explore the possibilities of how we can help each other in this space in which we are meeting. So, when a husband does not see his wife, he is unlikely to appreciate her. When an employer does not see employees, the company is unlikely to pay them a good living wage. When entrepreneurs don't see customers, they are likely to exploit them."[10]

And yet, as Mamabolo is quick to point out, when we *do* see people for who they are and acknowledge them through *Sawubona*, we are bestowing one of the greatest honours on another human being, filling them with hope and inspiration.

IN TORONTO, at the intersection of two very busy streets, there is a coffee shop.

The shop is next door to my office, and the very first time I went inside, the young woman who served me wore a badge with the name Alison.

Every time I saw this woman over the next two years, I greeted her, "Hey, Alison, how are you doing?"

Alison would smile and pour me a perfect double espresso, and we'd both go about our days.

Then one day, while I dropped in for a coffee on my way to work, Alison told me it was her last day. She had decided to leave that job. She turned to me with a conspiratorial glance.

"You know, I have to tell you something, Bill," she said. "The very first day you met me, I didn't have my name badge for work, and because we have to wear a name tag as a part of our uniform, my boss handed me someone else's to wear. My name isn't Alison, but I didn't have the heart to tell you."

What not-Alison didn't know was that my sister's name is Alison. It was really easy for me to remember her name. I just looked at her and thought, "you're my sister." And whenever I called her Alison, she smiled.

Not-Alison knew the truth about our connection. I'm sure her colleagues were asking, "Why does he keep calling you Alison?"

But that was our thing. That was our little bit. Even though I got not-Alison's name wrong every single time, it made her smile.

Not-Alison and I would chat almost every day. We laughed. We even cried over spilled milk together when one of her colleagues had a collision with a flat of two per cent.

It was our connection that bound us together, not her name tag.

TIP: See people. And notice the things around them that may be important.

Here's what I know.

In its simplest form, communication may be defined as the transmission of information and meaning from a sender to a receiver. It is something we do to bridge the distance between people, ideas and values.

For me, communication is being understood in the way that we intended to express ourselves. I love my sister

Alison (Ali) and my brother-in-law Bob. They communicate so clearly. One day I was with them on a gorgeous, sunny Kamloops day. Bob walked into the room and said to Ali, "It's a gorgeous day out there!" Ali's response? "We're *not* going golfing." Bob smiled and walked out of the room to do his chores. I laughed so hard. The message was delivered and completely understood. That's communication!

Employers, now more than ever, are requiring potential employees to converse with clarity; communication skills are the cornerstone of effective problem solving, and are useful in both personal and professional settings. You probably agree that the average manager wants to support open dialogue and for people to express their concerns and possible solutions to workplace problems. We all likely understand the idea that, especially in the business world, individuals need to adequately convey information essential to day-to-day functions. Messages need to be planned and executed professionally, in a way that expresses that they come from a knowledgeable and trustworthy source.

Or maybe not.

I'm not sure that so-called effective communication requires absolute clarity, skill or strategy.

What effective communication takes is effective *relationships*.

One day, when I was working at a bank, I walked past one of my employee's desks and noticed he had put up a picture of his daughter and her soccer team. What did I choose to do with that information? Let it go? Or pay attention?

"I notice that Julie is on a soccer team. When's her next game?" I asked.

"Oh, actually, it's tomorrow afternoon at three o'clock."

"Well, why don't you get out of here at two o'clock tomorrow and go and enjoy the game?"

That was all Julie's dad needed to hear. He went to the game, and when he came back to work the next day, he was more intrinsically motivated to engage. Would he work harder? My belief was, yes, of course. Because I acknowledged him as a human being.

TIP: Find what's special about the people you work with. Let them know what you value.

What's the distance between where you are and where you want to be? It's connection. And it's not just about building connections with other people.

It's about creating an authentic connection with yourself.

In the same spirit as *Sawubona*, I believe that everyone we interact with should feel special, valued and important (SVI).

Special means that we ought to see the uniqueness in everyone we meet and work with. When we walk into our office, we need to tap into what is different about each individual, rather than see them as the same flavour of customer service agent as the person sitting at the desk next to them. Everyone actually *is* special! Their experiences, ideas and personal history make them exciting to learn about as a whole human being.

Valued means that we need to be able to appreciate and articulate why someone's uniqueness is important to us. I want each person I work with to know why I value them. Out of all the things that make a person special, what delights you the most about them? Does the person who makes your sandwich at the lunch shop down the street pick great music? Does your co-worker have a knack for pointing out risks that need addressing so that a project doesn't fail? Does that person know how much you appreciate them?

Important means that everyone is seen and heard, without question. Their opinions matter, even when they're difficult to hear, or even if they're not in a managerial position. Everyone is worth our time, especially if they're asking for help.

WHY IS all of this critical?

Because for each of us to *really, truly* show up, we have to bring our whole selves. And we want to encourage everyone around us to do the same thing.

We can't just show up with our bodies, because, well, we'd be walking zombies.

We can't just show up with our minds, because we wouldn't get very far. And we'd be completely overthinking things and never accomplishing anything.

What we really need in order to show up is our spirits. Our essence. Our value systems and our psychologies, with all of their quirks.

When we treat people as special, valued and important, we are giving them the gift of psychological safety in our presence.

Psychological safety, as author Amy Edmondson explains, is the ability to create trust and mutual respect leading to a sense of security.[11]

In a project called Aristotle, Google tried to test what facets of work allowed teams to work well together. Based on data analysis of 51,000 employees, Google found that, more than anything else, psychological safety was critical to team effectiveness.[12] But, perhaps unsurprisingly, Google didn't really *get* how to translate this knowledge into action. They contacted their employees and discovered that the heart of psychological safety was, well, empathy. It was about forging a deeper, more meaningful social connection.

What all of this means is that treating people as SVI shouldn't be a goal.

It should be a baseline.

Nobody wants to pretend when they come to the office. And, of course, nobody wants to pretend at home. If we want people to feel as if they can express themselves and be fully present with us, we have to give them the gift of feeling SVI. Psychological safety can increase what the psychologist Abraham Maslow identified as *peak experiences*, in which we can truly feel as if we are being valued for the work that we do or just being the *person we are*. It helps us regulate our emotions, calm our nervous systems[13] and just *be*.

Remember when I told you that there was a time in my life where I *just knew* that I wanted to work at Disney?

Disney has a knack for making everyone feel amazing, from their customers to their employees. In fact, they state explicitly that their goal is to encourage people from every nation, race, ethnicity, belief, gender, sexual identity, disability and culture to feel respected and valued for their unique contributions. Behind the scenes, Disney has forty-five business employee resource groups representing eight dimensions of diversity in order to ensure that each team member feels included and resourced, including their Equality Institute for LGBTQ employees, founded more than twenty years ago. Disney has made inclusion a priority by recognizing the need for a sense of belonging in every person who interacts with the company in any way.

TIP: Create a safe space for

people—zero judgement.

Simply put, according to Disney, *starting every interaction with inclusion reminds us all—from fans to employees—that we belong.*[14]

That's why, when we go to places like Disneyland or watch a Disney film, we're swept away to a place where we become immersed in magic. We feel safe enough to let go and truly enjoy ourselves, because we're treated like we belong. We are welcome to be ourselves. We are given a passport into a place that values our uniqueness and yet allows us to join a club that includes millions.

SVI is the same kind of idea, but without the mouse ears.

Making people feel SVI is the process of breaking down as many barriers as possible between you and *every person you meet*, so that both they *and* you feel seen.

It can feel a little risky, I know. Especially in the last few years, we're so used to being on the alert for danger that making people feel SVI may feel like stretching a new muscle. And we have to respect boundaries! Not everyone will feel safe to *accept* being treated SVI, at least not at first.

But, let's face it. Our workplaces make it tough sometimes to practice seeing each other. Competition is fierce! Although most managers refer to their employees as teams, we all know on some level that we're being asked to compete for titles, resources, our managers' time, recognition, pay and job security, every single day. Employees aren't being seen as often as they'd like. In fact, research shows that there are companies with leaders who worry when employees spend even eighty minutes a week in social conversation,[15] as if this is something that ought to be of deep concern. If we spend eighty minutes talking to each other *over a whole week*, some employers perceive this as a bad thing!

Whether we're at home or at work, though, we have to check these assumptions, and our own fears. Think about it: would you rather compete or collaborate? Disconnect or connect? I think what we've all learned over the course of the pandemic, at the very least, is that human connection matters. That we should be open to listening when a person wants to express their feelings, be heard and seen, and to take steps to make that possible so that human connection *can* happen.

If we can start turning outward and invite a deep witnessing and presence with each other, we can create more mutual security, more innovation and more peak experiences. All in all, we can create more happiness.

SVI makes *belonging* possible.

When I offer someone an opportunity to connect, I feel personally rewarded. Just like walking through the gates at Disneyland, something magical happens, and whatever that interaction may be, I can't think of an occasion when a bit of human connection didn't feel like an amazing gift.

10

LIVE GIVING

The art of the hidden
law of reciprocity

THE NEXT time you're offered candy at a restaurant, you might want to think twice.

And I'm not talking about urine mints. (You *did* know that there's a significant amount of urine on those unwrapped restaurant after-dinner mints, bowls of which are stirred by the unwashed hands of hundreds of urinators, right?)

In the 1980s, Robert Cialdini, a professor at Arizona State University, looked at the way in which diners at a restaurant responded to receiving candy on a dish with their unpaid bill. He found that if a server gave the bill to the customer without any candy, they would receive a normal-range tip. If a server gave the bill to the customer *with* candy, they would also receive a normal tip, but a little on the higher side.

If the server forgot to give candy to the customer with the bill, but then returned to the table a few moments later, giving the diners some candy with an apology, the server would get a *bigger* tip. An exceptional tip.

Cialdini concluded that there is a hidden law of reciprocity in which people feel obliged to provide discounts or concessions to others if they've received favours from those same people. Human beings are wired to treat others as they've been treated. It's a social kindness thing.[16]

What I get from this social kindness law of reciprocity is that people may believe, under the surface, that if they've done something nice for someone else, they deserve something in return. This is a problem: this is a feeling of entitlement. It's not a connection between one person and another, but an expectation of a transaction.

You see, Robert Cialdini isn't just a psychologist. He's also a professor of *marketing*. And his work on the law of reciprocity is based on commercial interactions that lean heavily on human niceties. But the challenge is that his work helps companies to *exploit* these niceties, not create *real relationships*.

We've gotten so used to these kinds of transactions, that we can't always see the forest for the trees. And restaurants are often where the law of reciprocity is most readily on display. You're not only tricked by the candy switcheroo, but you know just what's happening when a server squats down to talk to you, winks and sweetly calls you and your dining mate "you guys!"

There's nothing wrong with marketing. But, in today's hyper-marketed world, we now expect that when we get a gift, there's actually a hidden hook placed inside to reel us back in; we feel we've been marketed to.

WHAT IF we can give gifts as our authentic, true selves and not our manipulative, forced selves? What if we expect nothing in return? What if we can give for the sake of giving?

Why? Because giving *feels good*.

And let's be clear. I'm not talking about birthday presents. We've all been under that particular pressure, especially when it comes to our closest family members and friends. If you give someone something they don't want, or the wrong thing, you weren't paying attention. And then that gift actually becomes offensive. Right? "I told you ten times I wanted blue Nikes, Mom! What are you doing giving me a red pair of Reeboks? How many times did I send you the link? How did you miss that?"

When it comes to gifts, what I am talking about is how to create positive, life-giving energy between two people.

TIP: Give—it feels good! Don't expect anything in return! Don't keep score!

Don't give a present. *Be present.*

The neurologist and author Viktor Frankl, who spent part of his life in a Nazi concentration camp, makes a convincing argument that it is possible to find meaning in our lives no matter what challenges we face in our day-to-day existence. He writes that there is meaning in suffering. He saw a way forward through the pain of his existence in the camp by creating space for meaning, even in the smallest of acts, through his interactions with others.[17] He and others he knew were able to imagine a different future for themselves than the one that they were experiencing.

And let's be real here. What Frankl reveals is that there's no such thing as altruism. What he did to help others helped him emotionally, psychologically and spiritually.

The media places a lot of social currency on humans being martyrs: parents putting their kids' needs first, workers who put in that face-time overtime, first responders rescuing people in danger, people who donate their time and money for a good cause. But the opposite point of view is also needed! We should be heroes of our own making, and not martyrs. How far would a first responder get without an oxygen mask and a whole bevy of colleagues? Giving to others is part of what allows us to be resilient and thrive; it feels like sharing a special bond.

We can think about giving in terms of *benefitting ourselves*, and that's okay, because it's better for everyone if we all just admit it.

So give what you truly want to give, and get what you truly want to get out of life.

Meaningful activity can be found anywhere, from the workplace to the coffee shop to nature, and knowing what matters most to you helps you see beyond what's happening right now. If you have money, give money. If you don't, don't be a martyr to yourself. Do something else. If you have time, give your time and volunteer for an organization. If you're already overwhelmed, give that gift of time to yourself! If you know you've got a friend in crisis, ask how you can help. And maybe you don't want to do heavy lifting and fill boxes of food at the food bank, but you could read or sing to an elderly person.

In other words, don't go *for* a connection, go *with* a connection. What's inside you wanting to be shared?

Frankl believed that it was possible to be inspired by our own imaginations. If we have the imagination to see a number of different paths ahead, all with a range of probabilities attached to them, we can discover something amazing about ourselves.

This is *super important*.

If we can work on developing the skills we need to explore our own imaginations, we'll find that we also have the skills to be creative and become the creator of our own lives. We can foster a shared, connected existence based on anything we imagine.

But we need self-awareness to achieve this goal.

What is something that you, and only you, feel brilliant about?

————————————

TIP: Write down your *own* philosophy.

————————————

The Champ family in Georgetown, Ontario, decided to bring some cheer to its community by creating 201 birdhouses and placing them under community mailboxes, on footpaths to parks, outside long-term care homes, schools and the local hospital. They decided to do this to bring smiles to people who live in this community, located just outside of Toronto.

A local news network broadcast a story about a man who placed cash in and around bus stops and signposts on the street so that random strangers would get a boost.

I can keep going.

Epicurus, a Greek philosopher, believed that the definition of human happiness was to be able to seek pleasure, and that happiness was the highest good in life.

There are only three things Epicurus believed were necessary for happiness.

The first is freedom, in the form of self-sufficiency and the ability to make choices for ourselves.

The second is friendship, namely spending time with those we love and those who challenge us.

And the third is philosophy: the ability to study the meaning of life.

In giving of ourselves to others via connection, we meet all of these criteria. By sharing what's inside us, doing it freely rather than by obligation or by expecting a gift in return, we can be truly happy.

SEE
THE BACK
ROW

The art of finding
hidden voices

WHEN I first started hosting large conferences, the tech team would darken the hall lights as soon as the show was about to start.

This is very normal, I know. We're all used to sitting in the dark so that the focus is on the stage. That's where the action is: where people speak, dancers float and pianists tinkle.

I feel differently though. It all comes back to what I've been talking about throughout this book: I want people to feel svi. So when it's me on the stage, I want to see those faces in the audience! It's not that I want the lights fully up, because that's no fun at all, but a little soft lighting never hurt anyone. So the lights are dimmed to fifty per cent, and we're all in an intimate but visible setting.

So there I was, presenting at The Art of Leadership in my old stomping grounds of British Columbia. Four women sat in the front row, in Platinum seats. These seats are practically on the stage with me. And each one of these women had an expression on her face that ranged from neutral to negative.

Seeing those faces, I felt like I was already failing. I mean, it's literally my job to bring energy to the room. And I wasn't sure if it was me, if I was just not bringing it, or if it was just a collective case of resting jerk face (RJF). We all have RJF sometimes, but, you know, maybe I wasn't their favourite person. I'm not everyone's special friend, even when I want to be. And that's okay. But they unnerved me. Every time I looked out at the crowd, I felt like I was letting them down.

TIP: Let's all avoid RJF

(resting jerk face) if we can!

I felt my energy waver. I looked at the back row instead of the front, and people were laughing along with me. This helped a little, but my mind kept wandering and wondering: Was I doing my job well? Did I need these women's acceptance? What was I missing?

I'm not on stage for long sometimes, and, in this case, as the clock ticked closer to lunchtime, I felt a sense of relief at the coming end of my presentation. That is, until the producer of the conference told me to go grab my meal in the Platinum room.

In that room, there were only a few open seats, including one at a table with these same four women.

I sat down at the table. It was not a comfortable place for me to be. I had to be on stage again in less than an hour. So I decided that there was nothing left to do but just Sheryl

Sandberg my way through lunch and "lean in." Sandberg, in her book of the same name,[18] advocates for deep listening and leaning into a conversation when we need to gain clarity.

And so I listened, and learned.

One of the women, Daphne, had recently visited a sanctuary for elephants in Thailand. Many of the elephants had some sort of physical ailment; some had been terribly abused by their owners, some had simply been overworked in logging camps and left for dead, some literally had broken backs from being ridden by tourists, some had stepped on land mines... the list went on. The sanctuary purchased these elephants and provided meals, shelter and safety, along with their very own mahout—an individual responsible for the care of the elephant.

What Daphne found fascinating was the relationship between the elephant and the mahout. She told us that their relationship was entirely synergistic, complete with compassion and mutual respect. The elephant chose to stay with the mahout, who devoted his entire day to the elephant. The rules that come with this responsibility are relatively simple, starting and ending with maintaining the happiness of the elephant.

Honestly, I felt myself becoming judgemental. I had heard about elephant conservation places where so-called mahouts carried whips and not everything was as rosy as it seemed on the surface. But Daphne's story was compelling, so I held my tongue.

The elephant's movements, Daphne explained, seemed completely random at first. After she watched for a while, she noticed that, sometimes, it appeared like the elephant was leading the mahout to the next destination: the river, or another group of elephants. Other times, the mahout was in the lead, carrying delicious watermelons, with the elephant following eagerly behind. And then there were times when mahout and elephant walked side by side, with a mutual destination and a shared view of the trail. On the whole, nothing was rushed or forced—the elephant and mahout both embraced the role of leader and follower, and switched seamlessly between them without effort or struggle.

I am glad that, that day, I was leaning in. I was listening instead of speaking. I was seeing instead of asking to be seen.

TIP: Listen, ask questions, clarify and *then* respond.

We asked each other a number of questions based on this story, and based on the fact that we were at The Art of Leadership. After hearing about elephants and mahouts, do we truly understand the leader and follower roles? Do people play both roles, often simultaneously? Do we follow the first rule of the mahout, to maintain the happiness of our elephants? What would happen if we took another look at how important this shared aspect of leadership can be? And more importantly, when we (or our elephants) get off track, do we make it enticing to come back?

RJFs turned into smiles. Smiles turned into laughter. I turned into myself again, appreciating that I was allowed to learn, to be a part of a conversation bigger than myself.

Connecting with people *feels like home.* It energizes us because we find the link between our stories and our spirits. There's a shared foundation, even between those of us with entirely different lived experiences, that comes to the forefront and makes our next steps together easier to navigate.

If you don't have all the lights on in the room, you can't see the back row. But the same goes for the front row.

And, the same goes for *you*, yourself.

I think that the biggest challenge we have is to see ourselves for who we are rather than who we pretend to be when we're out in front.

And the divide between each of us isn't in how we see each other, but how we see ourselves. This is because we can't always imagine ourselves in a place of deference, or of adventure, or of innocence. We see ourselves as being in a spotlight, either because we think we deserve it or because we are scared. No matter what, that spotlight stops us from looking farther than the end of that stage.

But we can see ourselves in each other. In our shared stories and experiences, in what delights and excites us. In what matters to each of us. In our sadness and fear. When we can find that moment of courage to sit at a table where we know we will be uncomfortable, we can find others' voices, and our own voices as well: the voices that ask rather than tell. The voices that offer and understand and bridge. The true voices we often can't hear.

It's your task to find those hidden voices and in them, a source for new meaning.

12

CROSS THE RIVER

The art of being true
to your spirit energy

TWO MONKS travelling together arrived at a river with a strong current. As the monks prepared to cross the river, they saw an old, tired woman also attempting to cross. The woman turned to the monks and asked them if they could kindly help her cross to the other side.

The two monks glanced at one another; they had made a solemn pact that they would never touch a woman.

Then, without a word, the older of the monks picked up the woman, carried her across the river, placed her gently on the other side and carried on his way without looking back.

The younger monk couldn't believe what had happened. After catching up to his companion, he was speechless, and an hour passed without a word between them.

Two more hours passed.

Then three. Finally, the younger monk couldn't contain himself any longer.

"I cannot believe you picked up that woman and carried her across the river," he angrily confessed to his companion. "Why did you carry that woman on your shoulders?"

The older monk looked at him and simply replied, "Brother, I set her down on the other side of the river; why are you still carrying her?"

TIP: Retain your power—don't carry someone else's burden.

You may have heard this story before, and its lesson is pretty clear: when we hold on to things that don't serve us, they take up needed emotional space in our heads. But let's put a twist on the tale of the two monks.

Crossing that river was a moment of confluence.

Confluence means *flowing together*. At a confluence, one river is forever impacted by the other river. What happens when one river becomes polluted even though the other flows with pure mountain water? Where those two rivers meet, *all of the waters will become polluted*. Or let's think of it another way. When one river flows with pure mountain water down to the point of confluence, its force can *clean and clear* the muddy depths of the other river. Both, or either, can be true.

When the two monks met the old woman at the river, both of them were affected by the experience. The younger monk found his values questioned by the experience. The older monk found an opportunity to teach the younger monk something new, something that he needed to know.

Have you ever noticed how two individuals can deal with similar circumstances, but do very different things with the experience? For example, two people can work hard and expend the same amount of energy and resources to launch projects. They may even achieve similar results. At the same time, they may have different *reactions* to those results. If neither project truly takes off, one person may become bitter and blame others, while another person may use the experience as a way to learn and create future opportunities.

And now we're back to where we started. Remember *mindset*? We can have an open mindset and can flow with the river, or we can create a barrier through a fixed mindset. There are many situations in which we're not coming into confluence with clarity, that's for sure.

Think about the last time you went into a meeting, or even met your bestie for coffee, and thought to yourself: "I'm going to get right out of here as fast as I can, as soon as I've downed this cappuccino or finished my departmental report." Sometimes we freeze. Sometimes we're not thinking with emotional intelligence. Sometimes we need those defence mechanisms and we've got to take time for ourselves. So do that. Conserve your energy when you need to.

But what happens more often than not is that when we do have that conversation, *the act of confluence changes us*.

Let me give you an example. I used to be in charge of a department in the travel industry, and sometimes, as we all know, people just don't seem happy in their roles. It's not a culture fit, or a job fit, or maybe it's as simple as a timing fit. There are many reasons that jobs just aren't a fit, even when everyone is doing everything right.

Once I had a really wonderful experience letting someone *move on* from their job. And helping them do it.

Dierdre said to me, "Bill, this isn't the place for me, is it?"

And I said, "No, Dierdre, it's not."

Before she could start worrying, I changed the energy of the experience for her, and, by extension, for me.

"Let's work on your resumé. Let's practice some interviewing skills; let's find you a place that's right for you. This is not your work home, but we can find you a new one."

"You sound excited. Why?"

"Why am I getting excited for you? Because I'm going to see you take on a new role at a place where *you want to be*. What are some questions you're going to ask in the interview to ensure that the new job is the right fit? To find out what your new manager might be like, when the chips are down? I'm getting excited for you because you've learned a lot here, and the next step will be to bring you closer to your ultimate job."

Together, Dierdre and I shifted our energy away from the negative connotations of job loss, because that is really all that they are. Connotations. Perceptions. Interpretations. What she needed from me was the fire, the electricity that I could bring into confluence, so that we could find flow and *feel good* about what we were creating in this transitionary time. When we share our energy with others in this way, we get it back. Amplified.

We are constantly in a state of confluence with those around us. Confluence is about realizing what intrinsically motivates us, and paying attention to what intrinsically motivates other people, and going with *that* flow.

But sometimes, confluence is not about other people at all.

Sure, we are constantly in a state of confluence with those we meet. We can add to others' energy with our commitment, knowledge and joy. We can also bring our muddy waters and dampen their enthusiasm and add to their fears, as they can do for us. And then we might start to think: Are other people stealing our energy? Maybe! If the waters are always muddy, that feels like a problem.

TIP: Keep your river clean, and purify others'.

But maybe it's not.

Maybe we need to look at this analogy in a totally different way.

Confluence is also about how we bring *all of what we have learned* together.

In our river, we've got our crystal-clear intuition, potential energy, choice and luck.

We've got the nutrients of emotional intelligence, human connection, consciousness and curiosity.

We've got the depth of our lived experiences, our communities, the meaning in our lives and in our shared stories.

And sometimes there's a little mud in there, because our human lives are allowed to be messy and there are always going to be mis-takes.

It's here in our own river that we find our spirit energy.

What do I mean by spirit energy?

I'm talking about our true essence. Remember: this body is on loan, as are our minds. Our spirits carry on.

Our spirits are the *deepest us* about us. We know we have spirit energy when everything comes together and we feel like a fully realized *whole person*.

When we allow ourselves to pay attention, be brilliant and go deep, and we no longer feel just *fine*.

When we feel powerful in our own right.

When we no longer have to count on external validation at work (or at home) to keep moving forward.

When we allow ourselves to be aligned with the natural flow of our own river, we experience a resonant emotional, physical and mental humming.

When we have the ability to use our potential energy and translate it into *self-ful* action.

I want you to leave work *with energy*, so that you can live this one precious life beautifully, floating in your own personal hurricane. And if there *aren't* still reasons to be passionate about what you're doing every day, then something has to change. Remember: your energy can be converted to different forms, but it can't be created or destroyed.

I've given you twelve tiny steps forward.

Start by taking one. Show up!

The 12 Microsteps

A REMINDER

Part I: Pay Attention

STEP 1: Find Your Hurricane

- Keep a list of all of your accomplishments—a *done* list!

- Always have your resumé on your desktop and up-to-date.

- Volunteer your ideas! Be *honest*.

- Maintain a growth mindset—ask questions and diversify your thoughts.

- Remember *why* you're passionate about your job!

STEP 2: Choose Your Balloon

- Good luck/bad luck: always question which it is and seek the other perspective.

- Use your superhero power—be curious!

- What are the events, workplaces or social groups where you feel engaged and valued for your contributions?

- Who is in control of the conversations where you feel seen and heard?

- How can you rethink your environment, even in the smallest way, so that you feel more alive and energized?

- What are the things you want to have an impact in your life, and change your balloon? What are the things you want to remove from your life so that they don't change your balloon?

- How can you get one per cent more comfortable in your role at work?

STEP 3: "FINE" Is Not a Feeling

- Check *in* with yourself—how are you feeling?

- What kind of day is it? Thumbs up or thumbs down?

- How much of a thumbs-up or -down feeling are you sensing in your body right now?

- What's the effect that you're having on other people when you're feeling like this?

- Why are you choosing to feel your feelings? Can you choose to feel a different way? Focus on what makes you feel the way you want to feel.

Part II: Be Brilliant

STEP 4: Plug In

- Decide what *your* desired results are, at work and in life.

- What breathes life into you at work?

- *Give* the energy you want to receive!

STEP 5: Be Self-ful

- Take care of yourself—put on your own oxygen mask first.

- What gives you energy, out of the activities you choose yourself? Write this down.

- Get a good night's sleep; know how your body works best. Stay hydrated.

- Challenge yourself: What kind of energy are you leaving in the room?

STEP 6: Power Your Curiosity

- Know what you want and be honest, transparent and truthful about it.

- Gamify your work—make it *fun*! *Reward* your desired behaviour!

- *Ask* the questions—be curious!

STEP 7: Celebrate Mis-takes

- Make mis-takes. Just do it.

- Discover, by listening and thinking creatively, new and better ways of doing what you've always done.

- Remember: all of what makes us human has to come to work. All of what makes us human has to come home as well. All of what makes us human is perfect in its imperfection.

STEP 8: Practice Pausitivity

- Discover the truth and say it—own it.

- Take a pause and observe, whenever you want to, to make things better!

- Focus on what you *know*—your life experiences and what you've achieved and experienced in the past. If you could do it then—you can do it now.

Part III: Go Deep

STEP 9: Show Me You

- See people. And the things around them that may be important.

- Find what's special about the people you work with. Let them know what you value.

- Create a safe space for people—zero judgement.

- Start turning outward and invite a deep witnessing and presence with others.

STEP 10: Live Giving

- Give—it feels good! Don't expect anything in return! Don't keep score!
- Don't give a present. *Be* present.
- Write down your *own* philosophy.

STEP 11: See the Back Row

- Let's all avoid RJF (resting jerk face) if we can!
- Listen, ask questions, clarify and *then* respond.
- Find hidden voices and stories, and in them, a source for new meaning.

STEP 12: Cross the River

- Retain your power—don't carry someone else's burden.
- Keep your river clean, and purify others'.
- Self-acknowledge your growth.

SURVEY SAYS?!

QUESTION 1:
On a scale of 0–10, how often do you *show up* in body, mind and spirit for *yourself*?

0   1   2   3   4   5   6   7   8   9   10

QUESTION 2:
On a scale of 0–10, how often do you leave work with more energy than you arrived with?

0   1   2   3   4   5   6   7   8   9   10

QUESTION 3:
On a scale of 0–10, how often are you honest with yourself about your feelings?

0   1   2   3   4   5   6   7   8   9   10

QUESTION 4:
On a scale of 0–10, how often do you truly connect with people?

0   1   2   3   4   5   6   7   8   9   10

QUESTION 5:

On a scale of 0–10, how often are you self-ful?

| 0 | 1 | 2 | 3 | 4 | 5 | 6 | 7 | 8 | 9 | 10 |

QUESTION 6:

On a scale of 0–10, how often do you demonstrate curiosity?

| 0 | 1 | 2 | 3 | 4 | 5 | 6 | 7 | 8 | 9 | 10 |

QUESTION 7:

On a scale of 0–10, how often do you make positive (learning) mis-takes?

| 0 | 1 | 2 | 3 | 4 | 5 | 6 | 7 | 8 | 9 | 10 |

QUESTION 8:

On a scale of 0–10, how often do you practice pausitivity?

| 0 | 1 | 2 | 3 | 4 | 5 | 6 | 7 | 8 | 9 | 10 |

QUESTION 9:

On a scale of 0–10, how often do you treat people as special, valued and important?

| 0 | 1 | 2 | 3 | 4 | 5 | 6 | 7 | 8 | 9 | 10 |

QUESTION 10:

On a scale of 0–10, how often do you feel true happiness?

| 0 | 1 | 2 | 3 | 4 | 5 | 6 | 7 | 8 | 9 | 10 |

QUESTION 11:

On a scale of 0–10, how often has your opinion changed when you truly listen rather than talk?

0   1   2   3   4   5   6   7   8   9   10

QUESTION 12:

On a scale of 0–10, how often do you truly *show up* in your full spirit energy?

0   1   2   3   4   5   6   7   8   9   10

ACKNOWLEDGMENTS

WHERE DO I begin? This book has been inside me for decades and getting it out was a daunting task. I could never have done it without my birth family and family of choice.

First, to my mother and father, who breathed life into me—you've been gone from this earth for too long, yet you're in my life every day.

Alice Margaret Foster Williams, your love and courage taught me so much.

Colin Harold Williams, you were an amazing man who constantly surprised me, especially in your later years, with your love and acceptance.

My sister, Alison, and brother-in-law, Bob, you are always there for me, and I love you more than you can ever know.

To some of the best leaders I've worked with, you showed me the way. To some of the worst managers I've worked with, you taught me how to never treat people and how I never wanted to let my team feel. To my favourite team member of all time, Dawn Frail. You're the ISTJ to my ENFP!

Christopher and Emily Novais, you forever changed my life the evening we shared a bottle of Dom Pérignon and you asked me to emcee your wedding. That was my first opportunity to really show you what I could do.

Christopher Novais and Scott Kavanagh, who partnered with me at The Art of Leadership, you had confidence in me to host your events. I am forever grateful for that first opportunity to host The Art of Sales in Vancouver and then The Art of Leadership and The Art of Leadership for Women in Toronto. You gave me the opportunity to meet so many amazing thought leaders who have truly inspired and influenced me, leading me to where I am today.

A short list of those speakers from whom I've learned so much: Dr. Tasha Eurich, Amanda Lang, Valerie Jarrett, Malala Yousafzai, Laura Gassner Otting, Robin Roberts, Neil Pasricha, Marcus Buckingham, Liane Davey, Sir Ken Robinson, Dr. Vince Molinaro, Tammy Heermann, Arianna Huffington, Kirstine Stewart, Susan David, Orlando Bowen, Geena Davis, Heidi Grant, Michael Bungay Stanier, Dr. Marshall Goldsmith, Eric Termuende, Dr. Shimi Kang, Dr. Robyne Hanley-Dafoe, Shawn Kanungo, Marnie McBean . . . okay so this is not a short list.

Thanks to Ron Tite, who introduced me to the amazing team at Page Two! Trena White, from the moment we connected I knew you and the team could get me through this. It wasn't easy and I cannot thank you all enough. To Lisa Thomas-Tench, a phenomenal writer—you found my voice and partnered with me to get the words on the page. To Amanda Lewis, an incredible editor who held my hand through the final edits . . . Thank you also to Melissa Kawaguchi, Jennifer Lum, Fiona Lee and Chris Brandt.

To my most important customers, you give me purpose; I hope you find this book helps you and your teams leave work with even more energy than you arrived with.

To Christian Lloyd and Ryan Wolman, you always challenge me, reflect how I may be appearing and make me look good as my authentic self.

To my guide, Stephen Westfall, you ground me and help me show up!

And one last thank-you, to you, the reader. I truly hope and trust that this book will help you pay attention, be brilliant and go deep.

Thank you all.

ELECTRIC BILL

NOTES

1   Carol S. Dweck, *Mindset: The New Psychology of Success* (New York: Ballantine Books, 2007).

2   Tasha Eurich, *Insight: Why We're Not as Self-Aware as We Think, and How Seeing Ourselves Clearly Helps Us Succeed at Work and in Life* (New York: Crown Business, 2017).

3   Daniel Goleman, *Emotional Intelligence: Why It Can Matter More Than IQ* (London, UK: Bloomsbury, 1996).

4   Patricia L. Lockwood et al., "Neurocomputational Mechanisms of Prosocial Learning and Links to Empathy," *Proceedings of the National Academy of Sciences of the United States of America* 113.35 (2016): 9763–9768, doi.org/10.1073/pnas.1603198113.

5   Kim Scott, *Radical Candor: How to Be a Kick-Ass Boss without Losing Your Humanity* (New York: St. Martin's Press, 2019).

6   Susan David, *Emotional Agility: Get Unstuck, Embrace Change, and Thrive in Work and Life* (New York: Penguin, 2016).

7   Sarah Donovan, C. Dominik Güss and Dag Naslund, "Improving Dynamic Decision Making through Training and Self-Reflection," *Judgment and Decision Making* 10.4 (2015): 284–295, journal.sjdm.org/14/14411/jdm14411.html.

8   M.M. Yang, Y. Zhang and F. Yang, "How a Reflection Intervention Improves the Effect of Learning Goals on Performance Outcomes in a Complex Decision-Making Task," *Journal of Business and Psychology* 33.5 (2018): 579–593, doi.org/10.1007/s10869-017-9510-0.

9   Ruth Helyer, "Learning through Reflection: The Critical Role of
    Reflection in Work-Based Learning (WBL)," *Journal of Work-Applied
    Management* 7.1 (2015): 15–27, doi.org/10.1108/JWAM-10-2015-003.

10 Roche Mamabolo, "Sawubona, We See You," TEDxMahikeng,
    September 23, 2019, youtube.com/watch?v=xpqU9MtL8MI.

11 Amy C. Edmondson, *The Fearless Organization: Creating
    Psychological Safety in the Workplace for Learning, Innovation, and
    Growth* (Hoboken, NJ: John Wiley & Sons, 2018).

12 Charles Duhigg, *The Power of Habit: Why We Do What We Do and
    How to Change* (New York: Random House, 2013). For more on Project
    Aristotle, see Google's "Guide: Understand Team Effectiveness,"
    re:Work (blog), rework.withgoogle.com/print/guides/5721312655
    835136/.

13 Nan (Tina) Wang, Traci A. Carte and Ryan S. Bisel, "Negativity
    Decontaminating: Communication Media Affordances for Emotion
    Regulation Strategies," *Information and Organization* 30.2 (2020):
    100299, doi.org/10.1016/j.infoandorg.2020.100299.

14 "Diversity, Equity & Inclusion," Walt Disney Company, 2021,
    thewaltdisneycompany.com/diversity-inclusion/.

15 Simon Linacre, "Time Well Spent? Differing Perceptions of Breaks
    at Work," *Human Resource Management International Digest* 24.3
    (2016): 11–13, doi.org/10.1108/HRMID-02-2016-0020.

16 Robert B. Cialdini, *Influence: Science and Practice* (Boston, MA: Allyn
    & Bacon, 2001).

17 Viktor E. Frankl, *Man's Search for Meaning* (Boston, MA: Beacon Press,
    2006).

18 Sheryl Sandberg, *Lean In: Women, Work, and the Will to Lead* (New
    York: Knopf, 2013).

ABOUT THE AUTHOR

"I never thought I'd follow in my father's footsteps.
But here I am, the son of an electrician, messing
with the same wiring in a different machine."
BILL G. WILLIAMS

HE'S CALLED "Electric Bill" for a reason. Bill G. Williams is on a mission to shock us out of our static daily routines. He is known for his unique brand of electrified methodologies for the workplace, and is now offering them to you in this book.

Bill's honest, succinct and enthusiastic approach to leadership has inspired and reshaped countless national organizations over thirty years. Whether coaching an individual over Zoom, or speaking to rooms of over a thousand delegates, Bill's impact is equally felt. His power comes from hearing "No" and reformulating it as "Not Yet."

Bill is the principal and president of the boutique leadership development firm The b⁴ Group Inc., and the host and brand ambassador for The Art of Leadership and The Art of Leadership for Women. Bill caters his solution-based strategies to individuals and corporations in the private, public and not-for-profit sectors.

This is Bill's first book. Tap into his energy; it's positively electric.

BILLGWILLIAMS.COM

READY TO AMP UP YOUR ELECTRIC LIFE?

Here Are Three More Ways to Plug In

Get *Electric Life* for your team or company: Share the buzz and connect your workplace! Purchase *Electric Life* for your team and I'll share my specialized content presentation with step-by-step discussion points to bring out everyone's full potential. Or go bigger and electrify your whole company; contact me directly for organization pricing, custom print runs that include messaging from senior officers and your own branding, and supplementary support content.

Get Bill as a keynote speaker: Let me bring the book to life with my unique brand of electricity, live on stage or at your online conference. Keynotes and Q&A sessions, customized and tailored with supplementary follow-up material, will help shock your organization out of negative patterns and make a measurable, positive difference to your work culture.

Get trained: Bring your organization or leadership team to its highest charge with *Electric Life* training sessions that are perfectly customized to your workplace. Online or in person, single or multi-day sessions; contact me and we'll find the best way to take your company to new levels.

Let's Get Electric Together

- ✉ bill@billgwilliams.com
- ⊙ @b4billgwilliams
- in Bill G. Williams
- ⊕ billgwilliams.com
- 💬 #ElectricLifeBook

CPSIA information can be obtained
at www.ICGtesting.com
Printed in the USA
BVHW031328290322
632742BV00003B/94